HIS MIGHTY
MIRACLES

OTHER BOOKS AND AUDIOBOOKS
BY SUSAN EASTON BLACK

400 Questions and Answers about the Book of Mormon

400 Questions and Answers about the Old Testament

*400 Questions and Answers about the
Life and Times of Jesus Christ*

400 Questions and Answers about the Doctrine and Covenants

Women of Character

Men of Character

Glorious Truths about Mother Eve

Glorious Truths about Mary, Mother of Jesus

Glorious Truths about Emma Smith

Glorious Truths about Women of the Restoration

The Other Martyr: Insights from the Life of Hyrum Smith

Alexander Doniphan: Courageous Defender and Friend of the Saints

HIS MIGHTY
MIRACLES

SUSAN EASTON
BLACK

Covenant Communications, Inc.

Cover image *Diverse Diseases* © J Kirk Richards. For more information visit www.jkirkrichards.com

Cover design copyright © 2022 by Covenant Communications, Inc.

Published by Covenant Communications, Inc.
American Fork, Utah

Copyright © 2022 by Susan Easton Black
All rights reserved. No part of this book may be reproduced in any format or in any medium without the written permission of the publisher, Covenant Communications, Inc., P.O. Box 416, American Fork, UT 84003. This work is not an official publication of The Church of Jesus Christ of Latter-day Saints. The views expressed within this work are the sole responsibility of the author and do not necessarily reflect the position of The Church of Jesus Christ of Latter-day Saints, Covenant Communications, Inc., or any other entity.

Printed in the United States of America
First Printing: October 2022

28 27 26 25 24 23 22   10 9 8 7 6 5 4 3 2

ISBN: 978-1-52442-249-3

To my son Todd,
a miracle in my life

CONTENTS

Introduction 1

Chapter One: Jesus Heals the Afflicted 5
   Healing a Nobleman's Son 5
   Healing Peter's Mother-in-Law 7
   Healing a Leper 9
   Healing the Centurion's Servant 11
   Healing the Paralytic Man 13
   Healing a Man with a Withered Hand 15
   Healing a Woman with an Issue of Blood 17
   Healing Two Blind Men 19
   Healing a Man near the Pool of Bethesda 20
   Healing the Deaf and Dumb 22
   Healing a Blind Man by Stages 23
   Healing a Blind Man on the Sabbath 25
   Healing a Crippled Woman 28
   Healing a Man with Dropsy 29
   Healing Ten Lepers 30
   Healing Two Blind Men (Bartimaeus) 32
   Healing the Ear of Malchus 33

Chapter Two: Jesus Casts Out Evil Spirits and Demons 35
   Casting Out an Unclean Spirit 36
   Casting Out Demons into Swine 37
   Healing a Man Possessed of a Devil 40

    Healing a Canaanite Daughter of an Unclean Spirit *41*
    Healing a Demonic Child *42*

Chapter Three: Jesus Raises the Dead **47**
    Raising the Daughter of Jairus *47*
    Restoring the Widow's Son *50*
    Raising Lazarus from the Tomb *52*

Chapter Four: Jesus Commands the Elements of Nature **57**
    Turning Water into Wine *57*
    First Miraculous Catching of Fish *59*
    Calming the Storm *60*
    Walking on the Water *62*
    Paying the Tribute Coin *64*
    Cursing of the Fig Tree *66*
    Second Miraculous Catching of Fish *68*

Chapter Five: Jesus Provides Food for Multitudes **71**
    Feeding the Five Thousand *71*
    Feeding the Four Thousand *74*

Chapter Six: Jesus Passes Unseen **77**
    Passing Unseen in Nazareth *77*
    Appearing to Two Disciples *79*

Chapter Seven: Jesus Achieves Universal Miracles **83**
    Performing the Atonement *83*
    Leaving the Open Tomb *86*

Conclusion **91**

INTRODUCTION

"Have miracles ceased because Christ hath ascended into heaven?" Mormon answered his own query: "Nay; neither have angels ceased to minister unto the children of men."[1] When my friends and I are asked, "Have miracles ceased?" we answer with Mormon, "Nay." We have each been blessed by miracles both great and small in a very personal recognition of our needs by an all-powerful, merciful God.

For example, I asked my sons, "What could we do for our next-door neighbor?" Even in asking, I wondered if anything was necessary. After all, Wasel Washburn had raised ten children and was a grandmother to many. Surely she had loved ones who would drop everything to help her.

"I will pick flowers from her window box and give them to her," Brian said. Todd, catching the drift of where the thought was heading, added, "I could shovel snow from her walks." It being mid-August, I was less than impressed with that suggestion. My youngest son, John, said, "I could bake her cookies." Cookies were baked and flowers picked, and Sister Washburn remained someone we waved to if she happened to be outside when we passed by.

Then came November, a change of weather, and a friendship. The friendship began when a few inches of snow covered the ground early on a November morning. I awoke Todd and said, "It snowed through the night." Being an avid skier, he replied, "I haven't waxed my skis." I told Todd, "Don't worry about waxing skis; our elderly neighbor needs her walks shoveled, and you said you'd do that."

Todd grudgingly put on his coat and walked out the side door. Within seconds, he was back in the house. "I can't shovel her walks," he said. "She has already shoveled them."

---

1 Moroni 7:27, 29.

"I'm embarrassed; we should all have helped her," I said.

With a big grin, Todd replied, "You think you're embarrassed? Look out the window."

Sister Washburn was shoveling *our* walks.

In that singular act of kindness, the stage was set for a miracle as Wasel Washburn and I became the best of friends. The miracle began when Todd asked his elementary school principal to call me because he felt sick and wanted to come home. The principal must have been busy, because a call was never made. Todd sat outside his office for a few minutes before heading home. He found the doors locked. He walked around the house, hoping to find an open window to climb through. When he reached the west side of the house, there stood my neighbor, waiting for him.

It was a Tuesday. Wasel had an assignment at the temple. She later told me that, while at the temple, she had an impression that she was needed at home. She left the temple immediately. After calling her family and finding all well, she walked out her front door and headed to my house to see if I needed help. She found my son Todd. She took him inside her home, fed him lunch, and together, they made rolls for me.

Through the next seventeen years, Wasel Washburn was my dearest friend, confidant, and adopted grandmother. As she neared her death in August 1993 at age ninety-six, I visited with her. The only thing she said to me was "Tell my boys I love them." I knew she was not talking about her sons.

I testify miracles still happen today. President Russell M. Nelson in his April 2021 general conference address advised, "Learn about miracles."[2] Wanting to know details of the miracles of Jesus, not just a broad brushstroke that affirmed my testimony, I studied the Savior's miracles. In the Gospels of Matthew, Mark, Luke, and John are thirty-eight miracles of Jesus written in narrative detail. These miracles have been the subject of theologians, academics, and Church leaders for centuries. In studying their works with the Gospels, I have discovered the miracles of Jesus fall into seven categories:

- Jesus heals the afflicted.
- Jesus casts out evil spirits and demons.
- Jesus raises the dead.
- Jesus commands the elements of nature.
- Jesus provides food for the multitudes.

---

[2] Russell M. Nelson, "Christ Is Risen; Faith in Him Will Move Mountains," *Liahona*, May 2021.

- Jesus passes unseen.
- Jesus achieves universal miracles.

Of these categories, six had an immediate impact—healing a blind man, turning water into wine, walking on the raging sea, and providing food for thousands. The universal miracles of Jesus had an immediate impact but also extended beyond the meridian of time. In a manner incomprehensible to me, Jesus took upon Himself the sorrow, suffering, and sin of all mankind from the days of Adam to the end of time. He then rose from the grave to conquer death so that all may live again. With the lyricist Charles H. Gabriel, I sing—

I stand all amazed at the love Jesus offers me,
Confused at the grace that so fully he proffers me.
I tremble to know that for me he was crucified,
That for me, a sinner, he suffered, he bled and died.
Oh, it is wonderful that he should care for me
Enough to die for me!
Oh, it is wonderful, wonderful to me![3]

I am not alone in being amazed at the love of the Savior. "Have miracles ceased because Christ hath ascended into heaven?" I asked a few friends.[4] The overwhelming response was "No." They then spoke of miracles great and small in their lives, revealing that the Lord has a very personal recognition of their needs. In this volume, discover not only details of the thirty-eight miracles from the life of Jesus Christ but also miracles in the lives of my friends. Dear reader, the Lord is also mindful of you. As you read this volume, take time to reflect and ponder on the miracles in your life and discover how the Lord has blessed you and your loved ones.

---

3 "I Stand All Amazed," *Hymns,* no. 193.

4 Moroni 7:27.

CHAPTER ONE
Jesus Heals the Afflicted

THE GOSPEL WRITER MATTHEW UNABASHEDLY declared that Jesus healed every sickness and every disease among the people, and He "healed them all."[1] We may never know the number of people healed by the Savior in Galilee, Capernaum, Perea, Gennesaret, or Jerusalem.

For example, when Jesus and His disciples arrived in the land of Gennesaret, word of the Lord's presence spread to the "whole region round about."[2] Inhabitants rushed to the Savior, bringing their sick, afflicted, and diseased on beds to "where they heard he was."[3] "And withersoever he entered, into villages, or cities, or country, they laid the sick in the streets, and besought him that they might touch if it were but the border of his garment: and as many as touched him were made whole."[4]

Of the thirty-eight miracles of Jesus recorded in some detail by Gospel writers, seventeen tell of miraculous healings.

HEALING A NOBLEMAN'S SON
John 4:43–54

Most Biblical scholars contend that St. John's account of healing the nobleman's son was the first healing miracle performed by Jesus and the second miracle of Jesus in Cana—the first being changing water into wine at a wedding feast. Note that even though the nobleman's son lay near death in Capernaum, the miracle is viewed as taking place in Cana.

---

1 Matthew 12:15.
2 Mark 6:55.
3 Mark 6:55.
4 Mark 6:56.

The story of this miracle began as "Jesus came again into Cana of Galilee. . . . And there was a certain nobleman" who had come seeking Him.[5] The nobleman had come from Capernaum, a lakeside community on the north shore of the Sea of Galilee. At that time, Capernaum was on the major international trade route between Damascus and Alexandria and boasted a population of five to six thousand residents. The fishing community was also a border station between Herod Philip's territories and the domain of Herod Antipas.

When the nobleman, an official of Herod Antipas, learned "Jesus was come out of Judaea into Galilee," he set out to find Him. The nobleman did not begin his plea before Jesus with mention that his son was of noble birth, nor did he put forward that his son was a lovely child. The nobleman had only one stated purpose in approaching the Master—"Heal his son: for he was at the point of death."[6] His errand was urgent.

Jesus responded to the nobleman's urgency by saying, "Except ye see signs and wonders, ye will not believe."[7] His saying was unexpected, for the nobleman did not ask for a sign. Yet the nobleman took no notice of the reproach, nor did he say anything by way of confession or excuse. Instead, he repeated his request: "Sir, come down ere my child die."[8]

In his urgency, the nobleman fell short of believing the divine promise in Psalms 107:20: "He sent his word, and healed them, and delivered them from their destructions." The nobleman thought the Master could not heal his son at a distance. Jesus corrected this misunderstanding by stating, "Go thy way; thy son liveth."[9] In His declaration, Jesus tested the nobleman's faith by asking him to believe His word alone, not an outward demonstration.

While in Cana, the nobleman did not see the dramatic change in his son's health. Yet he "believed the word that Jesus had spoken unto him, and he went his way. And as he was now going down [to Capernaum], his servants met him, and told him, saying, Thy son liveth."[10] The nobleman inquired "the hour when he began to amend. And they said unto him, Yesterday at the seventh hour the fever left him."[11] The nobleman "knew that it was at the same hour,

---

5   John 4:46.
6   John 4:47.
7   John 4:48.
8   John 4:49.
9   John 4:50.
10 John 4:50–51.
11 John 4:52.

in the which Jesus said unto him, Thy son liveth: and himself believed, and his whole house."[12]

The nobleman took his time returning home to Capernaum. When fear prevailed, the nobleman hurried from Capernaum to Cana. In faith, he now walked back to Capernaum, confident that his son was healed.

***

As my military departure date for Korea neared, I tried to get my orders changed to the States. I telephoned the base commander and said, "Please, sir, I don't want to go to Korea."

"Private Durrant," the commander said, "what kind of an army would it be if none of us were willing to go where we are needed?"

During my last days at Fort Smith, Arkansas, a doctor advised me that our baby Matthew needed an operation on a herniated navel. I knew a priesthood blessing was needed. A former missionary companion anointed my son, and I spoke the words of the blessing. I felt a miracle was occurring, but upon looking at my son's navel, his condition was the same.

After being shipped out to Fort Lewis to await a transport to Korea, I received this note from my wife: "I took the baby in for the operation. The doctor examined him and said, 'This baby doesn't need surgery. His navel is perfectly normal.'" It was then I knew that no matter what I faced in Korea, the Lord would care for my family.

—George D. Durrant, past director of priesthood genealogy in the Church

Healing Peter's Mother-in-Law
Matthew 8:14–15; Mark 1:29–31; Luke 4:38–39

Jesus healing Peter's mother-in-law occurred before Peter was called to be an Apostle of the Lord Jesus Christ. This was the first healing performed by Jesus on the Sabbath. Sabbath, derived from the Hebrew word *shabat*, means to "break off," "to desist," and "to rest."[13] On this holy day, devout Jews remembered and observed the goodness of God. Because of its holy nature, rabbis symbolically spoke of Sabbath as a bride. "All the days of the week,"

---

12 John 4:53.
13 Susan Easton Black, "The Sabbath as a Covenant in Mormonism and Judaism," in Raphael Jospe and others, eds., *Covenant and Chosenness in Judaism and Mormonism* (Madison, NJ: Fairleigh Dickinson University Press, 2001), 59.

the rabbis claimed, "has God paired, except the Sabbath, which is alone, that it may be wedded to Israel." Jews welcomed Sabbath as a groom greets with delight his bride and a nation rejoices in the advent of its king.[14]

On this particular Sabbath in Capernaum, Jesus taught in the synagogue and cast out an unclean spirit, revealing His authority over evil.[15] After services, the Master and His disciples Peter, Andrew, James, and John retired to Peter's home. There they discovered that "Simon's wife's mother was taken with a great fever."[16] Concerned about her health, the disciples "besought [Jesus] for her."[17] Jesus went into the room where the feverish woman lay and "stood over her, and rebuked the fever."[18]

Jesus "took [the woman] by the hand, and lifted her up; and immediately the fever left her."[19] St. Luke adds, "[The mother-in-law] arose and ministered unto them," meaning she resumed her responsibility of providing food and support for those in the house.[20]

***

I can truly say that the Lord's hand has blessed me all my life. The most recent series of blessings are the miracles I experienced producing *1820 the Musical*. The musical was slated to open May 2020 at BYU as part of the bicentennial celebration of the First Vision. The COVID-19 pandemic forced its cancelation. As I prayed for guidance to know how to proceed, the Lord guided me step-by-step from disappointment to fruition. He handpicked the perfect composers, choreographer, cast, and crew. He opened a theatre and the perfect rehearsal space.

As the rehearsal process was about to begin, I was diagnosed with stage-four esophageal cancer. Against the backdrop of this additional setback, I watched the Lord's hand move again to orchestrate things as only He could. My treatments, surgery, and hospitalization were woven into a timetable that allowed me to direct the show, oversee the installation in the theatre, and open

---

14   Alfred Edersheim, *The Temple: Its Ministry and Services, as They Were at the Time of Jesus Christ* (Grand Rapids, MI: Wm. B. Eerdmans Publishing Company, 1994), 177.

15   See Mark 1:21–26.

16   Luke 4:38.

17   Luke 4:38.

18   Luke 4:39.

19   Mark 1:31.

20   Luke 4:39.

the show on schedule. He even blessed my recovery enough to allow me to attend the closing night, wheelchair and all.

—George Nelson, professor in the Department of Theatre and Media Arts at BYU

Healing a Leper
Matthew 8:1–4; Mark 1:40–45; Luke 5:12–14

Jewish regulations required the leprous to stay at a distance from society. Lepers were expected to abandon their spouses and children and live with other lepers in dismantled houses or tombs east of the villages or cities in Palestine. If a leper dared approach a Jewish community, he was to warn all by crying aloud, "Unclean! Unclean!"

In this miraculous account, the leper defied social convention and regulations in a desperate attempt to get help. The leper came right up to Jesus and entreated Him to take away his affliction.

The story of this miracle began soon after Jesus taught His disciples on the Mount of Beatitudes. St. Matthew reported, "When he was come down from the mountain, great multitudes followed him."[21] When "he was in a certain city" near the Sea of Galilee, multitudes gathered to listen to Him.[22] Among them was a man afflicted with leprosy. The man not only listened to Jesus but also "fell on his face" and knelt before Him and "besought him, saying, Lord, if thou wilt, thou canst make me clean."[23]

The leper's faithful request was not uttered in a pretentious manner. His words reveal humility mixed with high expectations. His question was not, "Does Jesus have power to heal?" It was personal—"Will He heal me?" The question was urgent, for a man with leprosy was viewed as being punished for committing a grievous sin.

Jesus, seeing the man full of leprosy, was "moved with compassion."[24] He "put forth his hand, and touched him, and saith unto him, I will; be thou clean."[25] By the touch of the Master's hand, "he was cleansed."[26] Jesus charged

---

21 Matthew 8:1.
22 Luke 5:12.
23 Luke 5:12.
24 Mark 1:41.
25 Mark 1:41.
26 Mark 1:42.

the man, "See thou say nothing to any man: but go thy way, shew thyself to the priest, and offer for thy cleansing those things which Moses commanded, for a testimony unto them."[27]

Since the days of Moses, the law required all leprous men and women to show themselves to a priest and submit to ritualist cleansing before being readmitted into Jewish society. The ritualistic cleansing took place on the Temple Mount in Jerusalem. In the Court of the Gentiles, the cleansed leper gave an asham offering to a temple priest, a fine for not serving Jehovah due to physical impurity. The offering included "two birds alive and clean, and cedar wood, and scarlet, and hyssop."[28] The priest then monitored the shaving of the leper and examined the afflicted for signs of leprosy. If leprosy was not found, the cured man was quarantined for seven days and re-examined. If pronounced clean a second time, clothes of the cured were washed, a required temple sacrifice was offered, and blood from the offering was sprinkled on the altar. The man was then sprinkled with water from a pure flowing spring and welcomed back into Jewish society.

In this case, the cleansed man failed to heed Jesus's charge: "See thou tell no man; but go thy way."[29] According to St. Mark, the cleansed man "went out, and began to publish it much, and to blaze abroad the matter, insomuch that Jesus could no more openly enter into the city, but was without in desert places: and they came to him from every quarter."[30] St. Luke added, "To be healed by him of their infirmities."[31]

***

When I was about five years of age, a very small boy[,] I was crying from the pain of an earache. There were no wonder drugs at the time. . . . My mother prepared a bag of table salt and put it on the stove to warm. My father softly put his hands upon my head and gave me a blessing, rebuking the pain and the illness by authority of the holy priesthood and in the name of Jesus Christ. He then took me tenderly in his arms and placed the bag of warm salt at my ear. The pain subsided and left. I fell asleep in my father's secure

---

27 Mark 1:44.
28 Leviticus 14:4.
29 Matthew 8:4.
30 Mark 1:45.
31 Luke 5:15.

embrace. . . . That is the earliest remembrance I have of the exercise of the authority of the priesthood in the name of the Lord.32

—Gordon B. Hinckley

Healing the Centurion's Servant
Matthew 8:5–13; Luke 7:1–10

From the Mount of Beatitudes, Jesus headed to Capernaum, home to a Roman garrison of about eighty to a hundred men under the command of a centurion, a middling role in the hierarchy of the Roman army. "And when Jesus was entered into Capernaum, there came unto him a centurion, beseeching him."33

Every time a centurion is mentioned in the New Testament (seven times), the centurion is presented as an honorable man who recognizes the goodness of Jesus and His message of the kingdom of God. For example, it was a centurion who acknowledged Jesus on the cross as the Son of God, and it was the centurion Cornelius who became the first gentile convert.34

In this case, the centurion was a Roman officer and a Gentile. He had at his disposal soldiers recruited from Samaria and Caesarea. The centurion said to Jesus, "I am a man under authority, having soldiers under me: and I say to this man, Go, and he goeth; and to another, Come, and he cometh; and to my servant, Do this, and he doeth it."35

Yet the centurion looked upon Jesus not as an inferior in the occupied province of Palestine, but as a man worthy of respect with authority greater than his own. As the story of this miracle unfolds, the centurion (or his servants) address Jesus as "Lord."36 Willing to toss cultural norms aside, the centurion then expressed concern for a servant attached to his household "who was dear unto him, [and] was sick, and ready to die."37 The centurion asked for no sign but placed the issue in the hands of Jesus.

The centurion sought a cure for his servant but did not dictate to Jesus how to cure the man. His entreaty was followed by a delegation of Jewish

---

32   Gordon B. Hinckley, "My Testimony," *Ensign*, May 2000.
33   Matthew 8:5.
34   See Matthew 27:54; Acts 10.
35   Matthew 8:9.
36   See Matthew 8:8.
37   Luke 7:2.

elders who extolled the centurion's worthiness and spoke of his love for Israel: "For he loveth our nation, and he hath built us a synagogue."[38] In response to their entreaties, Jesus said, "I will come and heal him."[39] The centurion replied, "Lord, I am not worthy that thou shouldest come under my roof: but speak the word only, and my servant shall be healed."[40] In his statement, the centurion acknowledged being an outsider and a willingness to spare Jesus the uncomfortable decision of whether or not to enter a gentile residence.

"When Jesus heard these things, he marvelled at him, and turned him about, and said unto the people that followed him, I say unto you, I have not found so great faith, no, not in Israel."[41] Those who followed Jesus were unaccustomed to hearing the faith of a Gentile extolled. According to Jewish tradition, any Gentile was inferior to the least worthy in the house of Israel. Yet, in this instance and in the story of the Canaanite woman who appealed for her daughter's health, Jesus referred to a Gentile as having great faith.[42]

As the story continued, Jesus said to His disciples, "Many shall come from the east and west, and shall sit down with Abraham, and Isaac, and Jacob, in the kingdom of heaven. But the children of the kingdom shall be cast out into outer darkness: there shall be weeping and gnashing of teeth."[43] His message was a reiteration of what devout Israelites already knew—faith and righteousness are necessary to attain the kingdom of God.

Turning to the centurion, Jesus said, "Go thy way; and as thou hast believed, so be it done unto thee. And his servant was healed in the selfsame hour. . . . Returning to the house, [the centurion] found the servant whole that had been sick."[44]

Whether the centurion became a disciple of Jesus and followed Him in Palestine is unknown.

***

The other day my wife was sick; she came to me and requested me to pray to the Lord that she might be healed. The matter passed from my mind.

---

38   Luke 7:5.
39   Matthew 8:7.
40   Matthew 8:8.
41   Luke 7:9.
42   See Matthew 15:28.
43   Matthew 8:11–12.
44   Matthew 8:13; Luke 7:10.

The day following this I remarked to her that I had not seen her looking so well for some time previous. She replied, "I am perfectly sound." I had forgotten about her request that I should pray for her, and had not done so; but she was healed through her honesty, faith, and integrity towards the holy Priesthood. . . . She was healed by the power of God, without the laying on of hands. It was with that circumstance as it was anciently. "The centurion answered and said, Lord, I am not worthy that thou shouldst come under my roof; but speak the word only, and my servant shall be healed."[45]

—Heber C. Kimball

Healing the Paralytic Man
Matthew 9:1–8; Mark 2:1–12; Luke 5:17–26

St. Mark set the stage for healing the paralytic man by telling of Jesus again entering "into Capernaum after some days; and it was noised that he was in the house. And straightway many were gathered together, insomuch that there was no room to receive them, no, not so much as about the door: and he preached the word unto them."[46] Numbered among those listening to Jesus were Pharisees, scribes, and doctors of the law who had come from "every town of Galilee, and Judaea, and Jerusalem."[47] They had not come to be taught, but to criticize.

Hoping to join the crowded scene were four men bearing a litter on which lay a man afflicted with palsy. When the men were thwarted from entering the house where Jesus was, they sought another way "to bring him in, and to lay him before [Jesus]."[48] They resorted to an unusual expediency. The men carried the paralytic man to the rooftop, most likely using an outside stairway or ladder. They broke apart the roof by enlarging a trapdoor or breaking up tiles. To the crowd's dismay, the afflicted man was let down through the opening.

Although breaking up a roof appears extreme in our way of thinking, at the time, roofs were replaced after the rainy season. Thus, the removal of a roof was not unusual. However, the purpose for removing the roof was. Surely the four men believed Jesus could heal their friend. When Jesus saw their faith, He said to the paralytic man, "Son, be of good cheer; thy sins be

---

45   Heber C. Kimball, "Men ought to Practice what They Teach, etc.," in *Journal of Discourses*, 11:84.
46   Mark 2:1–2.
47   Luke 5:17.
48   Luke 5:18.

forgiven thee."[49] Note, Jesus first addressed the man's spiritual needs. He also said to him, "Son, be of good cheer."[50] This was the first time the Master used the phrase, "Be of good cheer." The second time was when the disciples saw Jesus walking on the Sea of Galilee, and the third, at the Last Supper when Jesus said to the disciples, "Be of good cheer; I have overcome the world."[51]

St. Mark turned the reader from the man forgiven of his sins to the scribes who reasoned "in their hearts."[52] The contrast between the friends of the healed paralytic and the scribes is compelling fodder for discussion. The friends had destroyed a roof to ensure their afflicted friend had access to the miraculous power of Jesus. The scribes and perhaps the Pharisees and doctors of the law did nothing but reason until asking, "Who is this which speaketh blasphemies? Who can forgive sins, but God alone?"[53] "And, behold, certain of the scribes said within themselves, This man blasphemeth."[54]

"When Jesus perceived their thoughts, he answering said unto them, What reason ye in your hearts? . . . Wherefore think ye evil in your hearts? But that ye may know that the Son of man hath power on earth to forgive sins, (then saith he to the sick of the palsy,) Arise, take up thy bed, and go unto thine house."[55]

Forgiveness of the afflicted was not visible, for no man but Jesus could verify the moment the man was forgiven. However, each in the crowd could verify the moment the man walked. As the man arose and took up his bed and walked among them, the crowd was amazed "and glorified God."[56]

***

The longer I live, the more I see acts of compassion from people around me as the Lord's miracles. People are placed around us to help in our hour of need. After black ice caused a rollover accident and severely injured our family and friends, I remember the kind, compassionate healthcare workers and community members who provided expert care and comfort to us. More recently, I think of dozens of people who contributed thousands of dollars to help our

---

49 Matthew 9:2.
50 Matthew 9:2.
51 See Mark 6:50; see Matthew 14:27; John 16:33.
52 Mark 2:6.
53 Luke 5:21.
54 Matthew 9:3.
55 Luke 5:22; Matthew 9:4, 6.
56 Matthew 9:8.

oldest daughter pay for radiation and chemotherapy for her brain tumor. Just as the Savior offers His grace, they freely offered to us what we could not provide for ourselves. Singer Julie de Azevedo Hanks penned a powerful song about our need to help each other as the Lord would: "We are the hands of heaven on earth, reaching out to each other through our good works. We know the Lord is there, and through us He can answer prayers. We are His hands, the hands of heaven on earth."[57] I join with her in testifying that we are the hands of heaven on earth.

—Devan Jensen, executive editor at the BYU Religious Studies Center

Healing a Man with a Withered Hand
Matthew 12:9–14; Mark 3:1–6; Luke 6:6–11

In a synagogue in Galilee, Jesus healed a man with a withered hand on the Sabbath. The narration of the miraculous healing was told by St. Luke: "And it came to pass also on another sabbath, that [Jesus] entered into the synagogue and taught: and there was a man whose right hand was withered."[58] On that holy day, Jesus was asked, "Is it lawful to heal on the sabbath days?"[59] The reason for the question was not to begin a discussion on proper observance of the Sabbath. The specific purpose was "that they might accuse him."[60] As to be expected, the scribes and Pharisees were those wanting to know the Master's answer. They were poignantly aware that rabbis allowed Sabbath healings to ward off death and just as aware that a withered hand was not life-threatening.

Jesus countered the poorly concealed purpose of their question by posing His own queries: "Is it lawful on the sabbath days to do good, or to do evil? to save life, or to destroy it?"[61] The scribes and Pharisees did not answer Him, for the Savior's questions were double-edged. To reply that it was lawful to do good on the Sabbath would be to justify the work of healing on the holy day. A negative answer would place the scribes and Pharisees in an uncomfortable alliance with evil.

With only their silence to go on, Jesus asked the same question another way: "What man shall there be among you, that shall have one sheep, and if it

---

57 Julie de Azevedo Hanks, "Hands of Heaven," *Come unto Christ: Values for Young Women* (CD).
58 Luke 6:6.
59 Matthew 12:10.
60 Matthew 12:10.
61 Luke 6:9.

fall into a pit on the sabbath day, will he not lay hold on it, and lift it out?"[62] Jesus answered His own query when the scribes and Pharisees held their peace. "How much then is a man better than a sheep?"[63] Jesus declared, "Wherefore it is lawful to do well on the sabbath days."[64] In His answer, Jesus revealed the hypocrisy of the scribes and Pharisees by pointing out their greater concern for an animal than an afflicted man.

Having compassion on the man with the withered hand, Jesus said to him, "Stand forth."[65] In obedience, the man arose. "Then saith he to the man, Stretch forth thine hand. And he stretched it forth" for all the worshippers to see.[66] His hand was healed "like as the other."[67]

Although the healed man's gratitude and that of the assembled was not recorded, the reaction of the Pharisees was. Disdain for the compassion and mighty power of Jesus hardened their hearts. They had no degree of reverence or gratitude for the miraculous. From that time forward, "the Pharisees went forth, and straightway took counsel with the Herodians against him, how they might destroy him."[68] In other words, the Pharisees entered into a league with men who aligned themselves with Herod Antipas to seek the death of Jesus.

***

Abe was seven and a half years old when he contracted a form of meningitis. For two months, he lay in his dark room wearing "blue-feety-pajamas." As he drank his meals through a straw, he grew weaker. Movement caused great pain. On one particular Sunday, as the rest of the family had gone to church, I talked with Abe about faith. I read to him Moroni 7:26: "Whatsoever thing ye shall ask the Father in my name, which is good, in faith believing that ye shall receive, behold, it shall be done unto you." Before I could say another word, Abe blurted out, "Why haven't you told me this, Mommy? God can heal me! I know He can! Mommy kneel down right now—I know I can be healed!" I tried to explain that it had to be the Lord's will, but Abe insisted. "Pray right now to heal me, Mommy!"

---

62 Matthew 12:11.
63 Matthew 12:12.
64 Matthew 12:12.
65 Mark 3:3.
66 Matthew 12:13.
67 Matthew 12:13.
68 Mark 3:6.

I kneeled down and humbly petitioned the Lord on behalf of my son, closing my prayer with, "Thy will be done." Immediately, Abe tried to sit up. Within twenty minutes, he was running down the driveway to welcome our family home from church.

—Lynn Hilton, instructor at the Stanford institute and co-founder of bookofmormoncentral.com

Healing a Woman with an Issue of Blood
Matthew 9:20–22; Mark 5:25–34; Luke 8:42–48

The miracle of healing the woman with an issue of blood occurred as Jesus was on His way to raise the daughter of Jairus. On that journey, a throng of people pressed against Him. Nevertheless, He moved forward until "a certain woman, which had an issue of blood twelve years" touched Him.[69] It is assumed the "certain woman" suffered from menorrhagia, a continuous menstruation. The Talmud prescribed astringents, tonics, and "carrying the ashes of an ostrich egg in a linen rag" as treatments for the ailment.[70] Jewish tradition demanded a woman with a flow of blood be secreted away or quarantined from society. Yet this woman boldly joined the throng that walked with Jesus.

Whether menorrhagia or another disease, the sickness had drained the woman of all her money: "[She] had suffered many things of many physicians, and had spent all that she had, and was nothing bettered, but rather grew worse."[71] Nevertheless, she did not stop trying to find a cure. When she heard that Jesus was in the press behind, she pushed with dogged determination through the crowd to touch His garment, "for she said, If I may touch but his clothes, I shall be whole."[72] The woman approached Jesus from behind and touched His outer garment. Her touch was rewarded, for "straightway the fountain of her blood was dried up; and she felt in her body that she was healed of that plague."[73]

Securing the desired blessing, the woman tried to escape notice by becoming one of many following Jesus to the home of Jairus. But "Jesus, immediately

---

69 Mark 5:25.

70 Susan Easton Black, *400 Questions & Answers about the Life and Times of Jesus Christ* (American Fork, UT: Covenant Communications, Inc., 2010), 119.

71 Mark 5:26.

72 Mark 5:28.

73 Mark 5:29.

knowing in himself that virtue had gone out of him, turned him about in the press, and said, Who touched my clothes?"[74] "When all denied, Peter and they that were with him said, Master, the multitude throng thee and press thee, and sayest thou, Who touched me?"[75] Jesus said, "Somebody hath touched me: for I perceive that virtue is gone out of me."[76] "And he looked round about to see her that had done this thing."[77]

When the healed woman "saw that she was not hid, she came trembling, and falling down before [Jesus], she declared unto him before all the people for what cause she had touched him, and how she was healed immediately."[78] If she had expected to be censured or chastised, such was not the case. Jesus addressed the woman with respect and kindness, calling her "Daughter" before saying, "Thy faith hath made thee whole; go in peace, and be whole of thy plague."[79] He also told her to "be of good comfort" and from that very hour "the woman was made whole."[80]

***

New Year's Eve is a terrible day to hear that your mother has only six months to live. Months of chemotherapy treatments had not been successful. While most people were celebrating the start of a new year, our family grappled with uncertainty, fear, and heartbreak. We prayed for a miracle.

Two years later, under the care of more optimistic doctors, Mom is still bravely trying different treatments. Some treatments work for a while, but none have proven entirely effective. I often wonder why Mom hasn't been completely healed—surely there could be no one more deserving of a miracle than she! But then I remember the kindness of family, neighbors, and friends who regularly visit, bring meals, or send messages of encouragement; the medicines and treatments that have slowed the cancer's growth; and the "bonus time" I have spent with her. I realize our family has been blessed with an abundance of miracles for which I am eternally grateful.

—Tiffany Taylor Bowles, associate director of education at the Church History Museum in Salt Lake City

---

74   Mark 5:30.
75   Luke 8:45.
76   Luke 8:46.
77   Mark 5:32.
78   Luke 8:47.
79   Mark 5:34.
80   Matthew 9:22.

Healing Two Blind Men
Matthew 9:27–31

The earliest account with attendant details of Jesus healing the blind is found in Matthew 9:27–31. The account closely follows the raising of the daughter of Jairus.

As Jesus walked the streets of Capernaum, two blind men followed behind crying, "Thou Son of David, have mercy on us."[81] In calling Jesus the "Son of David," the blind men witnessed their belief that Jesus was the Messiah. Jesus did not reject the title, object to their witness, or deny their appeal for mercy.

However, it was not until Jesus entered a house that the healing of the blind men occurred. It is assumed that He entered the home of Peter in Capernaum, where earlier He had healed a feverish woman. When the blind men entered the house, Jesus said to them, "Believe ye that I am able to do this?"[82] Without hesitancy or reluctance, they replied, "Yea, Lord."[83] Jesus then touched "their eyes, saying, According to your faith be it unto you."[84] With the touch of the Master's hand, "their eyes were opened."[85] The word *opened* in this case comes from an old Jewish expression meaning "to see." Jews often spoke of the blind having their eyes "shut." Jesus removed blindness so that what was closed to them visually was now open for the men to see and comprehend.

After healing the blind men, "Jesus straitly charged them, saying, See that no man know it."[86] The men had faith to be healed but not faith to obey the command. When they departed from the presence of the Master, they "spread abroad his fame in all that country."[87] Although their disregard for the word of Jesus cannot be condoned, their joy over the miraculous healing is admirable.

***

When I was in Paris, France . . . I had a dream that troubled me very much, in which I saw my first wife . . . lying sick at the point of death. And it so affected me that I awoke, being troubled in my feelings. I fell asleep again, and again the same scene presented itself to me when I again awoke and

---

81 Matthew 9:27.
82 Matthew 9:28.
83 Matthew 9:28.
84 Matthew 9:29.
85 Matthew 9:30.
86 Matthew 9:30.
87 Matthew 9:31.

experienced the same feelings of sorrow, and after some time slept again, and it was repeated a third time. I knew then that my wife was very sick, lying at the point of death. I got up and fervently prayed the Lord to spare her life until, at least, I should have another opportunity of meeting her in the flesh. He heard my prayer. . . . I feel consoled in knowing that she will be healed.[88]

—John Taylor

Healing a Man near the Pool of Bethesda
John 5:1–15

St. John tells of Jesus healing a crippled man near the Pool of Bethesda on a Sabbath day. The pool, located near a busy sheep market, was one of ten pools in Jerusalem. Only two pools are mentioned in the Gospels—the Pool of Siloam and the Pool of Bethesda. The double Pool of Bethesda, with its five porches and covered verandas, is the more famous of the two.

Within the porches of Bethesda "lay a great multitude of impotent folk, of blind, halt, withered, waiting for the moving of the water."[89] The afflicted superstitiously believed that "an angel went down at a certain season into the pool, and troubled the water: whosoever then first after the troubling of the water stepped in was made whole of whatsoever disease he had."[90] So intent were the sick and afflicted in watching the water that none looked to Jesus for deliverance.

Among the afflicted lying near the Pool of Bethesda was a crippled man who longed to be cured by the moving water. Taking notice of the man "which had an infirmity thirty and eight years," Jesus asked, "Wilt thou be made whole?"[91] "The impotent man answered him, Sir, I have no man, when the water is troubled, to put me into the pool: but while I am coming, another steppeth down before me."[92] "Jesus saith unto him, Rise, take up thy bed, and walk."[93] In His command, Jesus gave the man seemingly impossible challenges. Yet "the man was made whole, and took up his bed [a bed mat], and walked."[94]

---

88 John Taylor, "Funeral Discourses, etc.,"in *Journal of Discourses*, 22:354.
89 John 5:3.
90 John 5:4.
91 John 5:5–6.
92 John 5:7.
93 John 5:8.
94 John 5:9.

Certain Jews chided the man for carrying a bed on the Sabbath: "It is the sabbath day: it is not lawful for thee to carry thy bed."[95] Such action was a violation of Sabbath—an offense against law. Thirty-nine laws regulated the Sabbath, and the last prohibited carrying a load from one house to another. In the minds of the Jews, this man had committed a crime against the holy day.

Rather than owning the violation, the man presented an excuse for his actions: "He that made me whole, the same said unto me, Take up thy bed, and walk."[96] Then the Jews asked, "What man is that which said unto thee, Take up thy bed, and walk? And he that was healed wist not who it was: for Jesus had conveyed himself away."[97]

Jesus later found the man "in the temple, and said unto him, Behold, thou art made whole: sin no more, lest a worse thing come unto thee."[98] Jesus forgave the man's sins. Note the reversal of order in the miracle of the man healed of palsy at Capernaum and the man healed near the Pool of Bethesda. The palsied man was healed of his sins, then his affliction. The cripple at the Pool of Bethesda was healed of his infirmity, then his sins.

We might assume the man healed of palsy led a good life, but we might question the goodness of the man healed near the Pool of Bethesda, for he put Jesus in harm's way by telling "the Jews that it was Jesus, which had made him whole."[99] Learning that Jesus had healed the man, the Jews persecuted the Master and "sought to slay him, because he had done these things on the sabbath day."[100]

***

When my four-year-old son Adam was jumping from one couch to another, he smacked his face on the corner of a couch, causing his two front teeth to push inward. My wife gently pushed his teeth back in place. Almost immediately, the teeth looked gray. I gave Adam a priesthood blessing and promised him that his teeth would stay in his mouth until the proper time. Six weeks before turning age eight, Adam lost one of the "miracle teeth."

—Bryce Anderson, senior product manager of Digital Scriptures for the Church

---

95   John 5:10.

96   John 5:11.

97   John 5:12–13.

98   John 5:14.

99   John 5:15.

100   John 5:16.

Healing the Deaf and Dumb
Mark 7:31–37

When Jesus and His Apostles left the land of Tyre and Sidon, they journeyed "through the midst of the coasts of Decapolis" to the eastward region adjoining the Sea of Galilee.[101] As they walked along, great crowds followed them, including the lame, blind, dumb, and maimed. To the astonishment of onlookers, Jesus healed the afflicted: the dumb spoke; the maimed were made whole; the lame walked; and the blind received sight. The healed "glorified the God of Israel."[102]

Among the many healed was a man deaf and defective in speech. No mention is made as to how the man lost his hearing or how long he had suffered from a speech impediment. We only know that the man was brought to Jesus, and "they beseech him to put his hand upon him."[103]

The Master "took him aside from the multitude, and put his fingers into his ears, and he spit, and touched his tongue."[104] It could be said, "Jesus made use of the language of signs, because the man was deaf. He put his fingers in His ears, indicating that He would pierce through the obstruction. He touched his tongue, indicating that He would remove the impediment in his speech."[105] Accepting this explanation means that Jesus used signs to inform the deaf and dumb what parts of his body would be healed.

The miracle occurred as Jesus, "looking up to heaven . . . sighed, and saith unto him, Ephphatha, that is, Be opened. And straightway his ears were opened, and the string of his tongue was loosed, and he spake plain."[106]

When Jesus and the healed man returned to the crowd, Jesus "charged them that they should tell no man: but the more he charged them, so much the more a great deal they published it," for the multitude "were beyond measure astonished, saying, He hath done all things well: he maketh both the deaf to hear, and the dumb to speak."[107]

***

---

101   Mark 7:31.
102   Matthew 15:31.
103   Mark 7:32.
104   Mark 7:33.
105   John Roberts Dummelow, *A Commentary on the Holy Bible* (New York: MacMillan, 1909), 728.
106   Mark 7:34–35.
107   Mark 7:36–37.

[Following a car accident], I was on the operating table. . . . They sewed my upper jaw in place, and took fourteen stitches in my lower lip and lacerated cheek.

One of the attendants remarked, "Too bad; he will be disfigured for life." . . .

. . . Three very close friends, called and administered to me. In sealing the anointing, [one of them] said: "We bless you that you shall not be disfigured." . . .

The following October, . . . I sat at a table near where President [Heber J.] Grant was sitting. I noticed that he was looking at me somewhat intently, and then he said, "David, from where I am sitting I cannot see a scar on your face!" I answered, "No, President Grant, there are no scars."[108]

—David O. McKay

Healing a Blind Man by Stages
Mark 8:22–26

Not far from where Jesus fed five thousand on the plains of Bethsaida, He healed a blind man. Of the four detailed accounts of Jesus healing the blind, this miracle is unique in that it is the only instance in which Jesus healed someone in stages. There is no explanation given as to why the man was not healed all at once.

The miracle began as a blind man was brought to Jesus in Bethsaida. Family or friends of the blind man "besought [Jesus] to touch him."[109] Jesus agreed but did not touch the man in front of the piercing stares of what became a crowd. He took the blind man out of Bethsaida. When they were alone, Jesus put spittle on the man's eyes and placed "his hands upon him [and] asked him if he saw ought."[110] The man "looked up, and said, I see men as trees, walking."[111] Jesus then placed "his hands again upon his eyes, and made him look up: and he was restored, and saw every man clearly."[112] The phrase "he was restored" suggests the man had not been born blind.

Biblical scholars' opinions vary as to why the blind man was healed in stages. J. R. Dummelow reasoned, "Our Lord used this elaborate process because the man was a Gentile, and, therefore, was with more difficulty brought to believe

---

108   David O. McKay, "A Personal Experience of Divine Healing," comp. Claire Middlemiss, *Cherished Experiences: From the Writings of David O. McKay* (Salt Lake City: Deseret Book, 1970), 146–147.

109   Mark 8:22.

110   Mark 8:23.

111   Mark 8:24.

112   Mark 8:25.

and to understand."[113] James Harpur suggested the miracle was a learning opportunity for the disciples and that Jesus used the "miracle to embody the progressive enlightenment of the 'blind' disciples."[114] Mark Collins presumed the gradual healing

> shows that our spiritual enlightenment is a continuous process. At first, we cannot see God's truth clearly. Most of our spiritual blindness remains, but as our faith, obedience, and growth develops, Jesus, "the author and finisher of our faith" (Hebrews 12:2), increases the clarity of our spiritual vision through the power of His Holy Spirit. . . .
>
> . . . The fully restored sight proves that Jesus never leaves His work unfinished and that He performs it with excellence, the sterling attitude that should be present in all our actions and service.[115]

Whether these scholars are correct in their interpretation is unknown. What is known is that after the man's sight was restored, Jesus "sent him away to his house, saying, Neither go into the town, nor tell it to any in the town."[116] In other words, the man was to say nothing about how or who restored his sight.

***

Waited on my father again, who was very sick. In secret prayer in the morning, the Lord said, "My servant thy father shall live." I waited on him all this day with my heart raised to God in the name of Jesus Christ, that He would restore him to health, that I might be blessed with his company and advice. . . . At evening Brother David Whitmer came in. We called on the Lord in mighty prayer in the name of Jesus Christ, and laid our hands on him, and rebuked the disease. And God heard and answered our prayers—to the great joy and satisfaction of our souls.[117]

—Joseph Smith

---

113 Dummelow, *Commentary on the Holy Bible*, 728.

114 James Harpur, *Miracles of Jesus* (London: Reader's Digest, 1997), 66–67, as cited in Black, *400 Questions & Answers About the Life and Times of Jesus Christ*, 142.

115 Martin G. Collins, "The Miracles of Jesus Christ: Healing the Blind Man from Bethsaida," *Forerunner: God's Gift of Grace* (May–June 2012), vol. 21, number 3.

116 Mark 8:26.

117 Joseph Smith, in *History of the Church*, 2:289.

Healing a Blind Man on the Sabbath
John 9:1–12

On a Sabbath, as Jesus and His disciples entered the Holy City, they came upon a man blind from birth. The disciples asked Jesus, "Who did sin, this man, or his parents, that he was born blind?"[118] In their question, the disciples revealed the traditional Jewish belief that physical affliction was associated with sin and that children inherited the sins of their parents.

"Neither hath this man sinned, nor his parents," Jesus said, before explaining "that the works of God should be made manifest in him. I must work the works of him that sent me, while it is day: the night cometh, when no man can work. As long as I am in the world, I am the light of the world."[119] After He had spoken these words, Jesus "spat on the ground, and made clay of the spittle, and he anointed the eyes of the blind man with the clay."[120] Jesus then said to the man, "Go, wash in the pool of Siloam, (which is by interpretation, Sent)."[121]

The seven-word command was simple: "Go, wash in the pool of Siloam."[122] It required an obedient response. What if the blind man hesitated? What if he argued that nothing would be gained by going to the pool? Would the man still receive his sight? But the man did not hesitate to comply. He went to the Pool of Siloam, a pool of utmost significance during the Feast of the Tabernacles. As part of the feast, a Levite carried water from Siloam to the Temple Mount. The water, referred to as living water, was a reminder of flowing water from a rock in the days of Moses. It also symbolized a future messianic deliverance.[123]

At the Pool of Siloam, the man washed himself before returning to his accustomed place by the temple gate. Upon his return, "neighbours . . . which before had seen him that he was blind, said, Is not this he that sat and begged? Some said, This is he: others said, He is like him: but he said, I am he."[124]

When news spread through Jerusalem that the blind beggar could now see, he was asked, "How were thine eyes opened?" He answered, "A man that

---

118 John 9:2.
119 John 9:3–5.
120 John 9:6.
121 John 9:7.
122 John 9:7.
123 See Numbers 20:8–11; Isaiah 12:3.
124 John 9:8–9.

is called Jesus made clay, and anointed mine eyes, and said unto me, Go to the pool of Siloam, and wash: and I went and washed, and I received sight."[125]

Surely with such an honest answer the man anticipated others taking joy in his good fortune. Wanting to meet the man who had performed such a miracle, they said instead, "Where is he?"[126] The cured man said, "I know not."[127] This is the first of eleven times the word *know* is used in this story.

When townsfolk shared with the Pharisees that Jesus had opened the eyes of a blind man, the Jewish leaders were more interested in the crime of a cure taking place on a Sabbath day than the man receiving his sight. In speaking of what they perceived as Jesus's disregard for the holy day, some Pharisees mused, "This man is not of God, because he keepeth not the sabbath day." Others questioned, "How can a man that is a sinner do such miracles?"[128]

To reach a definitive conclusion, Pharisees approached the healed man. In an obvious attempt to undermine faith by assuring the man that Jesus had violated the Sabbath day and therefore could not be a man of God, they asked, "What sayest thou of him, that he hath opened thine eyes?"[129] The man answered, "He is a prophet."[130]

Not expecting such an answer, the Pharisees called for "the parents of him that had received his sight."[131] The man's parents did not want to get involved in what was becoming a heated discussion. Perhaps fearing retribution, they refused to be drawn into the debate. When the Pharisees asked, "Is this your son, who ye say was born blind? how then doth he now see? His parents answered them and said, We know that this is our son, and that he was born blind: but by what means he now seeth, we know not; or who hath opened his eyes, we know not: he is of age; ask him: he shall speak for himself."[132] In their answer, the parents affirmed the man was their son and was born blind. They refused to answer by what means he had his sight or who performed the miracle.

Unable to extract a contrary testimonial from the parents, the Pharisees again approached the healed man, saying, "Give God the praise: we know that this man [Jesus] is a sinner." The man answered, "Whether he be a sinner

125   John 9:10–11.
126   John 9:12,
127   John 9:12.
128   John 9:16.
129   John 9:17.
130   John 9:17.
131   John 9:18.
132   John 9:19–21.

or no, I know not: one thing I know, that, whereas I was blind, now I see."[133] The Pharisees asked, "What did he to thee? how opened he thine eyes?"[134] The man replied, "I have told you already, and ye did not hear: wherefore would ye hear it again? will ye also be his disciples?"[135]

Insinuating that the Pharisees wished to become disciples of Jesus was an insult the Jewish leaders could not abide. Angry at the man's impertinence, the Pharisees said, "Thou art his disciple; but we are Moses' disciples. We know that God spake unto Moses: as for this fellow, we know not from whence he is."[136] The man's response revealed his understanding of Jewish law: "Why herein is a marvellous thing, that ye know not from whence he is, and yet he hath opened mine eyes. Now we know that God heareth not sinners: but if any man be a worshipper of God, and doeth his will, him he heareth. Since the world began was it not heard that any man opened the eyes of one that was born blind. If this man were not of God, he could do nothing."[137] His rejoinder was an attack on the collective wisdom of the Pharisees. In anger, the Pharisees put the man in his place: "Thou wast altogether born in sins, and dost thou teach us? And they cast him out"—meaning the man lost fellowship in the synagogue.[138]

When "Jesus heard that they had cast him out; and when he had found him, he said unto him, Dost thou believe on the Son of God?"[139] The man asked, "Who is he, Lord, that I might believe on him? And Jesus said unto him, Thou hast both seen him, and it is he that talketh with thee. And he said, Lord, I believe. And he worshipped him."[140] Jesus taught him, "For judgment I am come into this world, that they which see not might see; and that they which see might be made blind."[141]

Overhearing their conversation, the Pharisees asked Jesus, "Are we blind also? Jesus said unto them, If ye were blind, ye should have no sin: but now ye say, We see; therefore your sin remaineth."[142] In other words, if the Pharisees had

---

133   John 9:24–25.
134   John 9:26.
135   John 9:27.
136   John 9:28–29.
137   John 9:30–33.
138   John 9:34.
139   John 9:35.
140   John 9:36–38.
141   John 9:39.
142   John 9:40–41.

been blind, they would have been guiltless, having an excuse for their behavior. Since they knew the scriptures and the law, they were guilty of offense.

***

September 6th.—This morning my attention was directed to Joseph Guy, a boy three years of age. . . . I went to see him in the afternoon: death was making havoc of his body; his former healthy frame was now reduced to a skeleton, and it was only by close observation we could discern he was alive. . . .

Sept. 7th. . . . We there called upon the Lord in solemn prayer, to spare the life of the child. . . .

From that hour he began to amend; and with a heart filled with gratitude to our heavenly Father, I am happy to say, that in a few days he left his bed, and joined his little companions.[143]

—Lorenzo Snow

Healing a Crippled Woman
Luke 13:10–17

There is only one account of Jesus preaching in a synagogue in the latter part of His ministry. His words in the Perea synagogue were followed by the healing of a crippled woman. In healing the woman, Jesus challenged the Jewish tradition regulating the Sabbath.

The miraculous healing began when He saw the crippled woman among the worshippers. St. Luke wrote that the woman "had a spirit of infirmity eighteen years, and was bowed together, and could in no wise lift up herself."[144] From Luke's description, we conclude the woman was suffering from a deformity—a curvature of the spinal vertebrae. She also "had a spirit of infirmity" and was bound by Satan.[145] Yet she did not neglect worship at the synagogue.

"And when Jesus saw her, he called her to him."[146] He did not wait for a petition for help. Instead, Jesus "said unto her, Woman, thou art loosed from thine infirmity. And he laid his hands on her: and immediately she was made straight, and glorified God" in fervent expressions of thanksgiving.[147]

---

143   Lorenzo Snow, "Organization of the Church in Italy," *Millennial Star*, Dec. 15, 1850; 371.
144   Luke 13:11.
145   Luke 13:11; see Luke 13:16.
146   Luke 13:12.
147   Luke 13:12–13.

Doubtless, many in the congregation rejoiced with the woman. But the ruler of the synagogue could not abide Jesus's seeming disregard of the Sabbath, for this holy day was "a sign between [God] and the children of Israel for ever" and bound Jehovah and His chosen people in a "perpetual covenant."[148]

The ruler attempted to turn the assembled from amazement at the power of Jesus to anger for violating the Sabbath. He "said unto the people, There are six days in which men ought to work: in them therefore come and be healed, and not on the sabbath day."[149] Jesus denounced the ruler for his sayings: "Thou hypocrite, doth not each one of you on the sabbath loose his ox or his ass from the stall, and lead him away to watering? And ought not this woman, being a daughter of Abraham, whom Satan hath bound, lo, these eighteen years, be loosed from this bond on the sabbath day?"[150] In other words, was not a daughter of Abraham, Isaac, and Jacob worthy of being healed on the Sabbath? Was she not of more value than an ox or an ass? "And when he had said these things, all his adversaries were ashamed: and all the people rejoiced for all the glorious things that were done by him."[151]

***

When Dad was diagnosed with COVID-19, he quarantined at home. By the time he agreed to go to the hospital, he had extensive lung scarring. That was on a Monday. By Tuesday, we were told he would need to be put on a ventilator. We reached out to family and friends and asked them to fast and pray for Dad. By Thursday, the oxygen needed to safeguard his life was reduced. We fasted again on Sunday. Although doctors told us Dad would be in the hospital at least a month or maybe two, he came home without oxygen the next Tuesday with no sign of scarring on his lungs. This was a miracle.

—Daniel (age 15) and Rose (age 17), high school students

Healing a Man with Dropsy
Luke 14:1–6

The last of seven miracles performed by Jesus on a Sabbath was observed by lawyers and chief Pharisees. St. Luke began the narrative by writing, "And it came to pass, as he went into the house of one of the chief Pharisees to eat

---

148 Exodus 31:16–17.
149 Luke 13:14.
150 Luke 13:15–16.
151 Luke 13:17.

bread on the sabbath day, that they watched him. And, behold, there was a certain man before him which had the dropsy."[152]

There are at least two reasons why the afflicted man may have entered the chief Pharisee's home. The altruistic reason would be in hopes of being healed. The sinister reason would be to tempt Jesus to perform a miracle on the Sabbath.

Although no one asked any questions, perceiving the thoughts of those present, "Jesus answering spake unto the lawyers and Pharisees, saying, Is it lawful to heal on the sabbath day?"[153] The query was not about whether the afflicted man should be healed but whether he should be healed *on the Sabbath*. Jewish leaders prided themselves on strict Sabbath observance and on other occasions had much to say about what was acceptable and what was not on the holy day. Yet to the question posed by Jesus, "they held their peace."[154]

Jesus healed the man suffering from dropsy "and let him go."[155] Perceiving disdain from Jewish leaders for His action, Jesus turned to His silent accusers and asked, "Which of you shall have an ass or an ox fallen into a pit, and will not straightway pull him out on the sabbath day?"[156] The Pharisees and lawyers refused to answer. Knowing their thoughts, Jesus rebuked their hypocrisy.

***

My mother picked me up from school. Before driving me home, she planned to stop at a gas station. Before we reached the station, Mom said, "We need to go home now." Pulling up to the house, I saw my dog, Snowball, by the side of the driveway. Snowball had been attacked by a coyote and was covered with blood. We carefully picked up my dog, and Mom drove to get help. If Mom had not listened to the still small voice, my dog would not have survived. In that moment, I knew the Lord loved me and Snowball.

—Andrew (age 15), high school student

Healing Ten Lepers
Luke 17:11–19

The miracle of healing ten lepers happened as Jesus and His disciples were passing through Samaria on their way to Jerusalem. When they "entered into

---

152 Luke 14:1–2.
153 Luke 14:3.
154 Luke 14:4.
155 Luke 14:4.
156 Luke 14:5.

a certain village [in Samaria], there met him ten men that were lepers, which stood afar off."[157] In a chorus of despair, the lepers "lifted up their voices, and said, Jesus, Master, have mercy on us."[158] Jesus said to the afflicted men, "Go shew yourselves unto the priests. And it came to pass, that, as they went, they were cleansed."[159] Although ten were cleansed and welcomed back into Jewish society, only one expressed gratitude to Jesus: "And one of them, when he saw that he was healed, turned back, and with a loud voice glorified God."[160] He then "fell down on his face" at the feet of Jesus and gave thanks.[161]

Jesus asked the cleansed man, "Were there not ten cleansed? but where are the nine?"[162] There had been a chorus of men asking for mercy, but when mercy was granted, nine failed to express gratitude. The healed leper did not answer the question, but Jesus and His disciples knew "there are not found that returned to give glory to God, save this stranger."[163] Jesus said to the stranger, "Arise, go thy way: thy faith hath made thee whole."[164] To be made whole is synonymous with being complete or made perfect.

***

A friend appealed to me, upon learning that the doctor had announced that his daughter, stricken with diphtheria, would die before morning. . . . I prayed with all the earnestness of my soul that God would heal that girl. While praying, the inspiration came to me: "The power of the living God is here on the earth. The Priesthood is here. Hurry! Hurry! . . . Go and rebuke the power of the destroyer, and the girl shall live." The doctor . . . could not refrain from expressing his surprise at the change in the girl's condition over night. The power of the living God rebuked the destroyer.[165]

—Heber J. Grant

---

157   Luke 17:12.
158   Luke 17:13.
159   Luke 17:14.
160   Luke 17:15.
161   Luke 17:16.
162   Luke 17:17.
163   Luke 17:18.
164   Luke 17:19.
165   Heber J. Grant, "An Illustration of the Destroyer Rebuked," in Conference Report, Apr. 1925, 9–10.

Healing Two Blind Men (Bartimaeus)
Matthew 20:29–34; Mark 10:46–52; Luke 18:35–43

Jesus and His disciples journeyed to Jerusalem on the Red Way or Bloody Path, a road named for violence robbers committed on unsuspecting travelers. When they neared Jericho, eight hundred feet below sea level and renowned as an oasis for travelers journeying between Galilee and Judea, their steps were arrested by the cry of a blind man.

Gospel writers Matthew and Mark report that Jesus healed two blind men as they were leaving Jericho to journey to Jerusalem. Luke counters with "as he was coming nigh unto Jericho."[166] The discrepancy may have something to do with two Jerichos at the time—the old and the new. The new Jericho was about two miles south of old Jericho. To leave old Jericho would be to come near new Jericho.[167] There is also the question of how many men were healed. Matthew reports two; Mark and Luke name one—Bartimaeus.

The story of Bartimaeus, son of Timaeus, began as he was begging on the Red Way near Jericho. As he heard a "multitude pass by, he asked what it meant."[168] He was told "Jesus of Nazareth passeth by."[169] Knowing that Jesus was in the multitude, Bartimaeus called to the Master, saying, "Jesus, thou Son of David, have mercy on me."[170]

The multitude rebuked the blind man for calling to the Master, telling him to hold his peace. Ignoring the rebuke, Bartimaeus "cried the more, saying, Have mercy on us, O Lord, thou Son of David."[171] The tenacity of Bartimaeus did not go unrewarded. "Jesus stood [or stopped on his journey], and commanded him to be brought unto him."[172] Without hesitancy, Bartimaeus "[cast] away his garment, rose, and came to Jesus."[173]

When Jesus asked him "What wilt thou that I should do unto thee?" he replied, "Lord, that I may receive my sight."[174] "And Jesus said unto him,

---

166 Luke 18:35.
167 Martin G. Collins, "The Miracles of Jesus Christ: Healing Blind Bartimaeus," *Forerunner: The Value of Wisdom* (May–June 2015), vol. 24, number 3.
168 Luke 18:36.
169 Luke 18:37.
170 Luke 18:38.
171 Matthew 20:31.
172 Luke 18:40.
173 Mark 10:50.
174 Mark 10:51; Luke 18:41.

Receive thy sight: thy faith hath saved thee."[175] St. Mark adds, "Go thy way; thy faith hath made thee whole."[176] Bartimaeus received his sight and followed Jesus, "glorifying God: and all the people, when they saw it, gave praise unto God."[177]

***

I was suddenly attacked with a slight fit of apoplexy. Next morning I felt quite comfortable; but in the evening at the same hour that I had the fit the day before, I was attacked with the most violent fever I ever experienced. The Prophet Joseph and Elder Willard Richards visited and administered unto me; the Prophet prophesied that I should live and recover from my sickness. He sat by me for six hours, and directed my attendants what to do for me. . . . My fever began to break, and it left me on the 18th day.[178]

—Brigham Young

Healing the Ear of Malchus
Luke 22:50–51

In the Garden of Gethsemane, Jesus was betrayed into the hands of temple guards and Roman soldiers by the traitorous kiss of Judas. Seeing their Master apprehended, the disciples called out, "Lord, shall we smite with the sword?"[179] The Apostle Peter did not wait for a reply. "Simon Peter having a sword drew it, and smote the high priest's servant, and cut off his right ear. The servant's name was Malchus."[180] Jesus said to Peter, "Put up thy sword into the sheath."[181] In other words, Jesus told him to return the sword to its scabbard.

To emphasize to Peter His voluntary submission, Jesus asked, "Thinkest thou that I cannot now pray to my Father, and he shall presently give me more than twelve legions of angels? . . . The cup which my Father hath given me, shall I not drink it?"[182] Drinking from a cup is a metaphor of Jesus's

---

175   Luke 18:42.
176   Mark 10:52.
177   Luke 18:43.
178   "The History of Brigham Young," *Millennial Star*, March 12, 1864; 167.
179   Luke 22:49.
180   John 18:10.
181   John 18:11.
182   Matthew 26:53; John 18:11.

willingness to submit to His Father and of the great burden His submission required.

When Peter did not answer, Jesus said, "Suffer ye thus far," meaning, permit even this. Then Jesus reached out His hand and touched Malchus's ear "and healed him."[183] Malchus's reaction to this very personal miracle was not recorded. Did he now question the betrayal of Judas and his own antagonism toward Jesus? Gospel writers do not provide answers.

Even though temple guards and Roman soldiers must have witnessed the miracle, they still led Jesus from Gethsemane to the antagonistic Jewish leaders waiting beyond the garden. As for the disciples, they scattered in fear.

***

In 2007 my mother was diagnosed with cancer. The news was devastating to her and to our family. She endured surgery, radiation, and chemotherapy. Our family prayed for her constantly. Fifteen years later, my mother is still with us and doing well. She is a blessing to our family and a living testimony to me that the Lord is a God of miracles.

—Mitchell J. Nelson, student at BYU–Pathway Worldwide

---

183   Luke 22:51.

CHAPTER TWO
Jesus Casts Out Evil Spirits and Demons

THERE WERE FIVE LIMITED MEDICAL practices available to the Jews at the time of Jesus—folk medicine, cultic healing, physician cures, magician's magic, and the ministrations of a miracle worker. Folk medicine consisted of traditional remedies passed from one generation to the next. Cultic healing was associated with specific locations believed to have healing properties, like the Pool of Bethesda. Physicians were available to those willing to be treated by a Greek or Roman surgeon. Greek physicians were more respected than their Roman counterparts. The wizardry of magicians was frowned upon by pious Jews but was a medical option. Magicians entreated the spirit world with incantations and secret herbs, hoping to cast out demons that caused affliction. The final medical option was a miracle worker.

Recognizing Jesus as a miracle worker, St. Mark wrote that "all the city [Capernaum] was gathered together at the door" and that Jesus turned none away.[1] "He laid his hands on every one of them, and healed them," even those "possessed with devils."[2] St. Matthew tells of "one possessed with a devil, blind, and dumb" being brought to Jesus, and He healed him.[3] St. Luke tells that "when the devil was gone out, the dumb spake."[4] Gospel writers recorded thirty-six references to demonic forces but only a few instances of those possessed by evil spirits being healed by the miraculous power of the Master.

---

1   Mark 1:33.
2   Luke 4:40; Mark 1:32.
3   Matthew 12:22.
4   Luke 11:14.

Casting Out an Unclean Spirit
Mark 1:21–27; Luke 4:31–36

On a Sabbath day in the busy fishing village of Capernaum, Jesus "entered into the synagogue."[5] It was the same synagogue that four future Apostles—Peter, Andrew, James, and John—prayed and worshipped Jehovah at. As Jesus taught, the assembled were "astonished at his doctrine: for he taught them as one that had authority, and not as the scribes."[6]

The story of the miracle began when "a man with an unclean spirit" cried out, "Let us alone; what have we to do with thee, thou Jesus of Nazareth? art thou come to destroy us? I know thee who thou art, the Holy One of God."[7]

In his outburst, the man revealed in the demonic world there are no atheists. Evil spirits know "Jesus of Nazareth" in His humanity yet recognize His deity as "the Holy One of God."[8] An ancient tradition claimed that knowing a name gave power over an individual. The wicked spirit, which had gained power to control the unfortunate man's actions and utterances, tried to overpower Jesus. The question, "Have you come to destroy us?" was an acknowledgement that the Messiah would destroy all satanic forces.[9]

Just a few verses before, Jesus had battled Satan and his temptations in the wilderness. Now, on a Sabbath day in a synagogue, where Israelites had gone to pray and worship, Jesus faced a satanic demonic force in the form of a man with an unclean spirit—a man who had lost control of his body to evil forces at enmity with God. Rather than let the man dominate the situation, "Jesus rebuked him, saying, Hold thy peace, and come out of him."[10] Why didn't Jesus want the demonic man to proclaim His divinity? Perhaps because such proclamations are not declarations of faith, and they do not lead to a converting testimony.

"And when the devil had thrown him in the midst, he came out of him, and hurt him not."[11] Those who witnessed the miracle "were all amazed, insomuch that they questioned among themselves, saying, What thing is this? what new doctrine is this? for with authority commandeth he even the unclean spirits, and they do obey him."[12]

---

5   Mark 1:21.
6   Mark 1:22.
7   Mark 1:23–24.
8   Mark 1:24.
9   Mark 1:24.
10 Mark 1:25.
11 Luke 4:35.
12 Mark 1:27.

This was the first of seven miracles in which Jesus cast out evil spirits and the first of three occasions when evil spirits gave polluted testimony that Jesus was the Anointed One.

***

When I was in England, brother Geo. D. Watt was the first man baptized. . . . The night previous to my going forward to baptize brother Watt and eight others, I had a vision, as old father Baker used to say, "of the infernal world." I saw legions of wicked spirits that night, as plain as I now see you, and they came as near to me as you now are, and company after company of them rushed towards me; and brother Hyde and brother Richards also saw them. It was near the break of day. . . . They came when I was laying hands upon brother Russell, the wicked spirits got him to the door of the room, I did not see them till after that took place, and soon afterwards I lay prostrate upon the floor. That was in England, pious England, in the little town of Preston. . . .

If evil spirits could come to me, cannot ministering spirits and angels also come from God? Of course they can, and there are thousands of them, and I wish you to understand this, and that they can rush as an army going to battle.[13]

—Heber C. Kimball

Casting Out Demons into Swine
Matthew 8:28–33; Mark 5:1–20; Luke 8:26–39

The narrative of this miracle provides the most detailed account in the Holy Bible of a man possessed by demons. The story of the man takes place near the Sea of Galilee in the Perean region, a region dominated by a gentile population. St. Matthew tells of Jesus coming to "the country of the Gergesenes" while St. Mark writes of His coming "into the country of the Gadarenes."[14] As the reader struggles to uncover which locale is correct, another dilemma is presented. Mark tells of Jesus coming "out of the ship" and being met by "a man with an unclean spirit."[15] Matthew tells of two men while Mark 5:2 reads "man."

Elder James E. Talmage wrote an apt description of the man with an unclean spirit:

> His frenzy had become so violent and the physical strength incident to his mania so great that all attempts to hold him

---

13 Heber C. Kimball, "Elders Called to Go on Missions, etc.," in *Journal of Discourses*, 3:229.
14 Matthew 8:28; Mark 5:1.
15 Mark 5:2.

in captivity had failed. He had been bound in chains and fetters, but these he had broken asunder by the aid of demon power; and he had fled to the mountains, to the caverns that served as tombs, and there he had lived more like a wild beast than a man. Night and day his weird, terrifying shrieks had been heard, and through dread of meeting him people traveled by other ways rather than pass near his haunts. He wandered about naked, and in his madness often gashed his flesh with sharp stones.[16]

Yet, such a man "when he saw Jesus afar off . . . ran and worshipped him."[17] He "fell down before [Jesus], and with a loud voice said, What have I to do with thee, Jesus, thou Son of God most high? I beseech thee, torment me not."[18] Jesus asked, "What is thy name?" He answered, "My name is Legion: for we are many."[19] Although the title "Legion" could be a reference to a division in the Roman army, especially since the insignia of the Roman military unit stationed in the region was a boar, Gospel writers took the position that the word "Legion" had more to do with the man possessed by "many devils" than a military division.[20]

Legion requested that Jesus not send them "out of the country," preferring to be sent into "a great herd of swine feeding" in the mountains above the sea.[21] "So the devils besought him, saying, If thou cast us out, suffer us to go away into the herd of swine."[22] The unclean spirits could not have chosen an animal more detested by the Jews than swine. Devout Jews never even spoke the word *swine*. To the Jews, swine represented anyone who trampled the word of God.

"Forthwith Jesus gave [the demons] leave. And the unclean spirits went out, and entered into the swine: and the herd ran violently down a steep place into the sea, (they were about two thousand;) and were choked in the sea."[23] Keepers of the swine "went their ways into the city, and told every thing, and what was

---

16   James E. Talmage, *Jesus the Christ* (Salt Lake City: Deseret Book, 1981), 310.
17   Mark 5:6.
18   Luke 8:28.
19   Mark 5:9.
20   Luke 8:30.
21   Mark 5:10–11.
22   Matthew 8:31.
23   Mark 5:13.

befallen to the possessed of the devils."²⁴ A multitude came to the seashore to see the man possessed of the devils. They were shocked to see him next to Jesus "sitting, and clothed, and in his right mind."²⁵ They were struck with fear that the man who had wandered naked about the tombs day and night was dressed and sane. The change in the man they once feared was dramatic, perhaps more so than swine rushing down the mountain to the sea. Instead of rejoicing that the man was free from demons, "the whole multitude of the country of the Gadarenes round about besought [Jesus] to depart from them; for they were taken with great fear: and he went up into the ship."²⁶

"And when he was come into the ship, he that had been possessed with the devil prayed him that he might be with him. Howbeit Jesus suffered him not, but saith unto him, Go home to thy friends, and tell them how great things the Lord hath done for thee, and hath had compassion on thee."²⁷ The man departed from Jesus and "began to publish in Decapolis how great things Jesus had done for him: and all men did marvel."²⁸ The healed man became a valued missionary throughout Decapolis, the region of ten cities—Seythopolis, Pella, Dion, Gerasa, Philadelphia, Gadara, Raphana, Kanatha, Hippos, and Damascus.

***

As a child I loved to sing "Tell Me the Stories of Jesus." I imagined His "blessings resting on me."²⁹ I loved the Old Testament story of an angel protecting Shadrach, Meshach, and Abednego in a fiery furnace.

When our family was young, we were engulfed in our own fiery furnace and helpless to save ourselves. We pled with the Lord for deliverance. In answer to our prayers, friends lifted us up and shared our burden. Advocates spoke in our behalf, even at their own peril. A loving Church leader traveled a significant distance to speak for us. He promised that if we focused on the Savior all would be well. Not only were we okay, but we were blessed beyond measure. Those who lifted us and dressed our wounds are now our dearest friends.

---

24 Matthew 8:33.
25 Mark 5:15.
26 Luke 8:37.
27 Mark 5:18–19.
28 Mark 5:20.
29 "Tell Me the Stories of Jesus," *Children's Songbook*, 57.

I have seen the Lord calm the fiery furnace. As a family, we have felt His hand bestowing blessings. The Lord has assured me of His lovingkindness.

—Matthew Chatterley, artist and educator

Healing a Man Possessed of a Devil
Matthew 9:32–34

After hearing that Jesus healed blind men in the village of Capernaum, men rushed to the Master, bringing their afflicted loved ones. Among the afflicted was "a dumb man possessed with a devil."[30] Jews superstitiously believed that if a man was unable to speak, he was possessed of a demon. If he could not speak his name aloud, the demon could not be removed. In other words, "a demon that made a man mute had cleverly prevented the revelation of the name of the demon inhabiting the victim, and therefore prevented the exorcism."[31]

For Jesus, the superstitious belief was not an impediment to healing the man. He summarily cast out the demon: "And when the devil was cast out, the dumb spake: and the multitudes marvelled, saying, It was never so seen in Israel."[32]

This miracle showed not only the power of Jesus over the demonic realm, but also the inherent weakness of Jewish superstition. The Pharisees failed to see that Jesus's power was from God. To them, His power was from Satan, and they said, "He casteth out devils through the prince of the devils."[33]

***

When asked by my mission president to train a Portuguese-speaking elder waiting for a visa to get into Brazil, I protested. I was barely comfortable speaking Spanish. Nevertheless, with my new companion, I got on a bus and settled in for a long ride to the city of Rivera. As my companion slept, I reminded the Lord that I had been called to the Uruguay-Paraguay Mission and that being expected to learn Portuguese was too much. Just as I dozed off, I heard a voice say, "I wouldn't have called you if you couldn't do it."

I was blessed with the gift of tongues. In Rivera, we taught Aristedes Acosta Ferrao, a man unlikely to accept the gospel. One day after Aristedes prayed,

---

30 Matthew 9:32.
31 David Guzik, "Matthew 9—Jesus Ministers and Heals," *Bible Commentary*, eduringword.com.
32 Matthew 9:33.
33 Matthew 9:34.

he yelled at me, "Get out! Get Out!" I felt as if light literally left the room. A priesthood blessing followed. Since his baptism, Aristedes served a mission in the Brazilia North Mission. He married in the São Paulo Brazil Temple and became the father of eight children, seven serving missions. I know the Lord is in charge of this great latter-day work.

—Craig Ainge, Ainge CPA Group LLC

Healing a Canaanite Daughter of an Unclean Spirit
Matthew 15:21–28; Mark 7:24–30

In the days of Jesus, Tyre was larger than Sidon and probably exceeded Jerusalem in population. Most residents of these gentile cities reveled in the pagan worship of Ashtoreth and Baal. Ashtoreth was revered as a goddess of sensual love and Baal was the pagan god of the Asiatic. To these imaginary gods, residents of Tyre and Sidon offered gifts and sacrifices, even child sacrifices, to appease the gods' shifting whims. Jews referred to their pagan worship as the worship of nonentities or figments of a distraught mind.[34]

When Jesus came "into the borders of Tyre and Sidon, [he] entered into an house, and would have no man know it: but he could not be hid."[35] The reason being, "he could not deny them; for he had compassion upon all men."[36]

One who came seeking His help was "a certain woman, whose young daughter had an unclean spirit, heard of him, and came and fell at his feet."[37] The woman was a Canaanite by birth, a Greek by heritage, and a Syrophoenician by nationality.[38] Yet the gentile woman cried unto Jesus, "Have mercy on me, O Lord, thou Son of David; my daughter is grievously vexed with a devil."[39] According to St. Matthew, Jesus "answered her not a word. And his disciples came and besought him, saying, Send her away; for she crieth after us."[40] Jesus said, "I am not sent but unto the lost sheep of the house of Israel."[41]

---

34 See Bruce R. McConkie, *The Mortal Messiah: From Bethlehem to Calvary*, 3 vols. (Salt Lake City: Deseret Book, 1980), 3:8.

35 Mark 7:24.

36 Joseph Smith Translation, Mark 7:24 [in Mark 7:24, footnote *a*].

37 Mark 7:25.

38 See Mark 7:26.

39 Matthew 15:22.

40 Matthew 15:23.

41 Matthew 15:24.

The woman would not be denied. She "worshipped him, saying, Lord, help me."[42] Jesus said to her, "Let the children first be filled: for it is not meet to take the children's bread, and to cast it unto the dogs."[43] (When bread was lifted from a tray, crumbs would fall to the floor. Just like today, household pets at that time would wait for the crumbs to fall.)

Jesus said to the Canaanite woman, "O woman, great is thy faith: be it unto thee even as thou wilt. And her daughter was made whole from that very hour."[44] When the woman returned "to her house, she found the devil gone out, and her daughter laid upon the bed."[45] As for Jesus, He departed from the gentile cities.

***

When I was nine years old, my family took a vacation to Hawaii. One day, my family went to the beach. I stayed in the rented condo. As time passed and my family didn't return, I went outside to find them. The door to the condo automatically locked behind me. I walked a short distance and thought I could find my way back. Because all the condos looked the same, I couldn't. I was lost and scared. A lady in a car stopped. Her name happened to be Angel. She looked a lot like my grandmother—even her dog looked like my grandmother's. She asked, "Are you lost?" I said, "Yes." She helped find my way back to the anxious arms of my mother. Her act of kindness was a miracle to me.

—Ben, high school student

Healing a Demonic Child
Matthew 17:14–20; Mark 9:14–29; Luke 9:37–43

Jesus climbed a high mountain to commune with God. He took with Him Peter, James, and John. There, on what has become known as the Mount of Transfiguration, the Apostles saw Jesus ministered to by ancient prophets.

The nine Apostles left in the valley were not as fortunate. They struggled, for they had given scribes reason to criticize their discipleship and their Master. Scribes had taken a decided offensive approach, and the Apostles took a defensive posture. The result was a disputation that engulfed not only the disciples and scribes, but also a multitude near the base of the mount.

---

42 Matthew 15:25.
43 Mark 7:27.
44 Matthew 15:28.
45 Mark 7:30.

Jesus, coming upon the scene of disputation, witnessed a great multitude surrounding His disciples and the disciples being questioned by scribes in a confrontational manner.

"And straightway all the people, when they beheld [Jesus], were greatly amazed, and running to him saluted him."[46] Jesus lost no time in fanfare. He turned to the scribes and, referencing His disciples, asked, "What question ye with them?"[47] At that moment, Jesus assumed the burden of the dispute no matter what the issue. In so doing, He relieved the distressed disciples from further questions. The scribes did not answer Jesus's questions. When confronting His disciples, they had not withheld criticism. When confronted by the Master, however, they fell silent.

It was "a man of the company [who] cried out, saying, Master, I beseech thee, look upon my son: for he is mine only child."[48] "Lord, have mercy on my son: for he is a lunatic, and sore vexed."[49] The boy's illness, be it epilepsy or lunacy, was viewed as a disgraceful disease. Those with a superstitious bent believed the illness was due to sin against the moon. For the superstitious, changes in the moon were thought to control epileptic and demonic possession. Although such notions were absurd, it took centuries to eradicate them.

As evidence of his son being "sore vexed," the father told Jesus that "ofttimes it hath cast him into the fire, and into the waters, to destroy him . . . Wheresoever he taketh him, he teareth him: and he foameth, and gnasheth with his teeth, and pineth away."[50] The father then told of bringing his son to the "disciples, and they could not cure him."[51]

"Jesus answered and said, O faithless and perverse generation, how long shall I be with you? how long shall I suffer you?"[52] Reproof in the Savior's words was directed to the nine Apostles who failed to heal the boy. His ministry was nearing a close, yet not even the Apostles, who had walked with Him and been by His side for years, understood His power. Jesus directed the afflicted lad be brought "hither to me."[53]

---

46 Mark 9:15.
47 Mark 9:16.
48 Luke 9:38.
49 Matthew 17:15.
50 Matthew 17:15; Mark 9:18, 22.
51 Matthew 17:16.
52 Matthew 17:17.
53 Matthew 17:17.

In the Master's presence, the demon threw his young victim into a terrible convulsion. The boy fell to the ground, wallowing in convulsive contractions that seemed to drain life from him. In contrast, with calm deliberation, Jesus "asked [the boy's] father, How long is it ago since this came unto him? And he said, Of a child. . . . Jesus said unto him, If thou canst believe, all things are possible to him that believeth. And straightway the father of the child cried out, and said with tears, Lord, I believe; help thou mine unbelief. When Jesus saw that the people came running together, he rebuked the foul spirit, saying unto him, Thou dumb and deaf spirit, I charge thee, come out of him, and enter no more into him. And the spirit cried."[54]

The demon "came out of him: and he was as one dead; insomuch that many said, He is dead. But Jesus took him by the hand, and lifted him up; and he arose."[55] Jesus delivered the boy to his father. The evil spirit entered no more into the lad.

When Jesus and His disciples left the base of the Mount of Transfiguration, they entered into a house. In the privacy of a home, the disciples asked, "Why could not we cast him out?"[56] Jesus did not cushion the answer—"Because of your unbelief: for verily I say unto you, If ye have faith as a grain of mustard seed, ye shall say unto this mountain, Remove hence to yonder place; and it shall remove; and nothing shall be impossible unto you."[57] Jesus added, "This kind [meaning what the young boy experienced] can come forth by nothing, but by prayer and fasting."[58] Jesus taught His Apostles that prayer and fasting give added strength to those receiving and giving blessings.

***

As a law professor teaching Biblical law in the 1990s, I became intrigued with an event reported in Jeremiah 32:11. It involved a land transaction and a deed subscribed by witnesses, having one portion "sealed" and the other portion "open," which was signed and buried in a container so that it would be preserved "many days," all according to some customary law. This intrigued me for reasons that should be obvious to Latter-day Saints.

---

54 Mark 9:21, 23–26.
55 Mark 9:26–27.
56 Mark 9:28.
57 Matthew 17:20.
58 Mark 9:29.

Reading that text launched me on a quest. I wondered: what kind of legal document was this? Checking the main commentaries on Jeremiah, I found no help. On my way to a conference on ancient Near Eastern law in the Netherlands, I stopped at libraries and museums in England, where I hoped to speak with friends. But again, they were of no help. In those pre-internet days, research was often hit-and-miss, mingled with serendipity.

Having arrived at the conference in Holland, I sat in the same chair all three days in the library room at the Institute of Papyrology where we met. Only on the last day did my eyes wander and notice the books on the shelves right behind my seat. On the spines of dozens of obscure publications and technical reports in various languages were titles about doubled, sealed witnessed legal documents—a legal practice in Israel around 600 BC to record terms of important legal transactions—just like the deed described in Jeremiah 32. I count this as a miraculous answer to my question, my quest, and my prayers.[59]

—John W. Welch, professor of law emeritus at BYU

---

[59] See John W. Welch, "Doubled, Sealed, Witnessed Documents: From the Ancient World to the Book of Mormon," in *Mormons, Scripture, and the Ancient World: Studies in Honor of John L. Sorenson*, ed. Davis Bitton (Provo, UT: FARMS, 1998), 391–444; and John W. Welch and Kelsey D. Lambert, "Two Ancient Roman Plates," *BYU Studies*, vol. 45, number 2 (2006), 54–76.

CHAPTER THREE
Jesus Raises the Dead

GOSPEL WRITERS SHARED THREE INSTANCES of Jesus miraculously restoring life to the dead—the daughter of Jairus, the widow's son at Nain, and the beloved friend Lazarus. The resumption of mortal existence was not a resurrection from death to immortality. It was a raising from death to mortal life.

RAISING THE DAUGHTER OF JAIRUS
Matthew 9:18, 23–26; Mark 5:21–24, 35–43; Luke 8:40–42, 49–56

After crossing the Sea of Galilee and reaching the shore near Capernaum, Jesus and His disciples were greeted by a multitude. Among their number were the sick and afflicted and those who had become disciples of the Master. But "behold," meaning suddenly and unexpectedly, there came to Jesus the ruler of the synagogue, Jairus.[1] Jairus had not come to greet Jesus; he had come to fall at His feet. His action was most unusual, for Jesus was viewed as an itinerant teacher by many, but not Jarius. This ruler, who was respected for his rank in Capernaum society, knew Jesus was more than an itinerant teacher.[2] By kneeling or falling at His feet, he acknowledged the superiority of the Master. His action also acknowledged a willingness to sacrifice prestige and respect to express love and concern for a daughter, "for he had one only daughter, about twelve years of age, and she lay a dying."[3]

In the presence of curious bystanders, Jairus besought Jesus "greatly, saying, My little daughter lieth at the point of death: I pray thee, come and lay

---

1 Luke 8:41.
2 See Matthew 8:5–13.
3 Luke 8:42.

thy hands on her, that she may be healed; and she shall live."[4] Jesus did not ignore the urgent plea, nor did he ask Jairus to wait while others on the shore received a healing blessing. The Savior responded immediately and went with the ruler to his home.

Although none could deny Jairus's faith in the healing power of Jesus, it could rightly be said that his faith did not mirror the centurion's, who viewed distance as no hindrance to the Savior's limitless power. Jairus viewed it necessary that Jesus be in his house for a miracle to occur.

As Jesus and His disciples proceeded to Jairus's home, "much people followed him, and thronged him."[5] Their steps were arrested when a messenger approached bearing sorrowful news. He said to Jairus, "Thy daughter is dead: why troublest thou the Master any further?"[6] Although death appears final—the victor over life—St. Mark tells us, "As soon as Jesus heard the word that was spoken, he saith unto the ruler of the synagogue, Be not afraid, only believe."[7] In other words, do not let the certainty of death destroy the belief that your daughter will be healed.

The contradictory message—life and death—dramatically changed Jairus's hurried manner. Whereas he had been urgent in his plea for immediate help, the emergency of his pleading faded. For example, as they continued to journey to his house when the woman with an issue of blood touched Jesus's garment and the Master stopped to converse with her, there was no hint of impatience or displeasure on the part of Jairus. When Jesus finally arrived at "the house of the ruler of the synagogue," He found "tumult, and them that wept and wailed greatly."[8] He saw and heard professional mourners and minstrels "making a noise"[9] with their flutes and other instruments. "And when [Jesus] was come in, he saith unto them, Why make ye this ado, and weep? the damsel is not dead, but sleepeth."[10] Jesus's use of the Old Testament metaphor of death being a form of sleep was not lost on the paid mourners. They "laughed him to scorn, knowing that she was dead."[11] Regarding this reaction, James E. Talmage wrote,

---

4 Mark 5:23.
5 Mark 5:24.
6 Mark 5:35.
7 Mark 5:36.
8 Mark 5:38.
9 Matthew 9:23.
10 Mark 5:39.
11 Luke 8:53.

His words drew scorn and ridicule from those who were paid for the noise they made, and who, if what He said proved true, would lose this opportunity of professional service. Moreover, they knew the maid was dead; preparations for the funeral, which custom required should follow death as speedily as possible, were already in progress.[12]

Ignoring the cultural norms, Jesus "put them all out."[13] "He came into the house [and] suffered no man to go in, save Peter, and James, and John, and the father and the mother of the maiden."[14] In the presence of these five witnesses, Jesus grasped the young maiden's hand and said, "Talitha cumi; which is, being interpreted, Damsel, I say unto thee, arise. And straightway the damsel arose."[15]

Jesus instructed her parents to give their daughter meat to eat, for she was still dependent on natural laws that required nourishment for the body. Jesus had raised the damsel from the dead, but when there were acts that others could do, He did not take their place.

The five witnesses were charged that "no man should know it," meaning the miracle was to be kept secret.[16] The reasons given for the injunction of secrecy are unknown. No matter whether the witnesses kept this miracle secret, news of raising the daughter of Jairus "went abroad into all that land."[17]

***

John K. Carmack and I were asked to give a priesthood blessing to Bishop John Koer, a patient in the St. John's Hospital in Santa Monica, California. After Brother Carmack anointed Bishop Koer, I started to pronounce a blessing and said, "I would like to bless you with health, strength, and freedom from pain, but I can't." Then a blessing flowed that I will never forget. The significance of that blessing to me came at the funeral of Bishop Koer. From the pulpit, Patriarch Orson Haynie said, "I am prompted to tell you of a blessing that I pronounced upon the head of John Koer." As he recounted the blessing, I was overcome, for it was the exact blessing I had given him through the inspiration

---

12 James E. Talmage, *Jesus the Christ* (Salt Lake City: Deseret Book, 1981), 314–315.
13 Luke 8:54.
14 Luke 8:51.
15 Mark 5:41–42.
16 Mark 5:43.
17 Matthew 9:26.

and guidance of the Holy Ghost. This experience prepared me for service in the kingdom of our Father in Heaven and to know the reality and blessing of the holy priesthood.

—William W. Tanner, dentist and publisher of *Pioneer Magazine*

Restoring the Widow's Son
Luke 7:11–17

Leaving Capernaum, a village on the northern shore of the Sea of Galilee, Jesus and His disciples walked in a southwesterly direction to a farming village at the northern end of Mount Moreh in the eastern Jezreel Valley. The village, known as the city of Nain, was off the beaten path. Access to the city was limited to a single dirt road. As far as is reported, no one had asked for Jesus to come to Nain. No one was expecting Him, but He definitely was en route.

St. Luke informed his readers that as Jesus "went into a city called Nain," He was accompanied by "many of his disciples . . . and much people."[18] The large company arrived in Nain in time to join a funeral procession. Leading the procession were women. Jews held the false belief that through a woman, death came into the world and each time death took a life, women were to lead the procession to the burial site.

In readiness for the funeral procession and subsequent burial, within hours of his death, not days, the deceased was washed and anointed with oil and wrapped in linen bands with myrrh and aloes placed within the folds.

As the funeral procession moved toward the burial site at the outskirts of town, the deceased was carried behind the women on a bier. Those carrying the bier frequently rotated to give several mourners an opportunity to perform a last act of kindness for the deceased. Behind the bier were a minimum of two flute players and, where money was not an issue, hired professional mourners. As the procession advanced to the burial site, all who witnessed the sorrowful scene were expected to join in. Therefore, it is assumed that Jesus and the large group accompanying Him participated.

When the procession reached the gravesite, the mourners stopped, for Jesus saw the widow and "had compassion on her, and said unto her, Weep not."[19] His admonition was curious, for it did not match the expected sorrow of a woman who had lost her son. Jesus did not wait for the widow or anyone else to plead with Him to raise the son from the dead. Isaiah prophesied that such

---

18   Luke 7:11.
19   Luke 7:13.

HIS MIGHTY MIRACLES 51

would be the case: "I am sought of them that asked not for me; I am found of them that sought me not."[20] Yet the widow was in need. In Jewish culture, when a husband died before old age, it was considered a manifestation of God's judgment against the widow. To have an only son taken also, the widow's sin was viewed as enormous.

With compassion, Jesus moved forward "and touched the bier: and they that bare him stood still. And he said, Young man, I say unto thee, Arise."[21] The young man arose, "sat up, and began to speak."[22] It was then that Jesus "delivered him to his mother."[23] Upon observing the deceased sit up and speak, "there came a fear on all: and they glorified God, saying, That a great prophet is risen up among us; and, That God hath visited his people."[24] Reports of the miracle in Nain were carried throughout the land. Because of this miracle, the fame of Jesus grew "throughout all Judaea, and throughout all the region round about."[25]

***

While researching the life of Karl G. Maeser, I became aware that an infant named Karl Franklin Maeser (born in January 1857) died on a journey from Liverpool to Philadelphia. For years, the Maeser family had tried to learn where the infant was buried but without success. Many descendants supposed the baby was buried at sea. I believed he was buried in Philadelphia.

On a trip back East to visit my family, I took a day to travel to Philadelphia. After stepping off the train, I walked to the city archives only to discover that due to funding cuts, the archives were closed. Since I had not been to Philadelphia before and there was much to see, I continued walking. As I was wandering past the Historical Society of Pennsylvania, I decided to go inside. It cost a membership fee to obtain access to their library. I paid the fee and perused their records.

Within fifteen minutes, I found the death record of the baby, the attending physician, and the name of the cemetery. Karl Franklin Maeser died on July 4, 1857, as the ship entered port, and was buried in the Machpelah Cemetery not far from the dock. I don't believe this discovery was an accident. It was a

---

20   Isaiah 65:1; see Romans 10:20.
21   Luke 7:14.
22   Luke 7:15.
23   Luke 7:15.
24   Luke 7:16.
25   Luke 7:17.

tender mercy from the Lord to me and a reminder that He who notices when a sparrow falls knows the details of our lives.

—Buddy Richards, president of the Provo City Center Temple

Raising Lazarus from the Tomb
John 11:1–45

The raising of Lazarus from the dead is only recorded in the book of John. It begins, "Now a certain man was sick, named Lazarus."[26] He lived with his sisters Mary and Martha in Bethany, a village on the Mount of Olives approximately two miles from Jerusalem.

Word of Lazarus being sick was sent to Jesus in Perea. When Jesus learned of his illness, He said, "This sickness is not unto death, but for the glory of God, that the Son of God might be glorified thereby."[27] Yet He did not immediately leave Perea. The book of John tells us, "He abode two days still in the same place where he was."[28] During those days, Jesus performed a healing on the Sabbath. He also shared with His disciples parables about wedding guests, a great supper, the lost sheep, a lost coin, and Lazarus and the rich man.[29]

It was not until two days had passed that Jesus said to His disciples, "Let us go into Judaea again."[30] In an attempt to remind their Master of the animosity toward Him in Judea, His disciples said, "Master, the Jews of late sought to stone thee; and goest thou thither again?"[31] Jesus answered, "Our friend Lazarus sleepeth; but I go, that I may awake him out of sleep."[32] Not comprehending the Old Testament metaphor, His disciples said, "Lord, if he sleep, he shall do well."[33] Clarifying their misconception, Jesus said "plainly, Lazarus is dead. . . . let us go unto him."[34] The first disciple to proclaim a willingness to return to Judea was Thomas. Although Thomas was later viewed as the skeptic in the apostolic circle, he was the disciple who said, "Let us also

---

26   John 11:1.
27   John 11:4.
28   John 11:6.
29   See Luke 14:1–4, 7–24; 15:3–10; 16:19–31.
30   John 11:7.
31   John 11:8.
32   John 11:11.
33   John 11:12.
34   John 11:14–15.

go, that we may die with him," revealing a willingness to suffer with Jesus should the Jews take Him and put Him to death upon His arrival in Judea.[35]

By the time Jesus and His disciples neared Bethany, Lazarus "had lain in the grave four days."[36] According to Jewish custom, Lazarus was buried on the day of his death. His body was wrapped in traditional burial clothes and laid in a private tomb. Burial places hewn in solid rock were used as sepulchres by the Jewish upper class. Those who died in poor families were buried in cemeteries.

Mourners had gathered at the home of Mary and Martha when Martha received news "that Jesus was coming." She "went and met him: but Mary sat still in the house."[37] Sitting was an outward display of grief.

Martha was in a hurry to greet Jesus. She ran eastward down the Roman road until she saw Him. She called out, "Lord, if thou hadst been here, my brother had not died. But I know, that even now, whatsoever thou wilt ask of God, God will give it thee."[38]

Jesus said to Martha, "Thy brother shall rise again."[39]

Martha replied with certainty that Lazarus "shall rise again in the resurrection at the last day. Jesus said unto her, I am the resurrection, and the life: he that believeth in me, though he were dead, yet shall he live: and whosoever liveth and believeth in me shall never die. Believest thou this?"[40] Martha professed her absolute faith—"Yea, Lord: I believe that thou art the Christ, the Son of God, which should come into the world."[41]

Without further comment, Martha distanced herself from Jesus and returned to "Mary her sister secretly, saying, The Master is come, and calleth for thee."[42] Mary arose and headed to the eastward approach to Bethany to greet her Master. She did not go alone. Family and friends who "were with her in the house, and [had] comforted her, when they saw Mary, that she rose up hastily and went out, followed her, saying, She goeth unto the grave to weep there."[43]

Mary went straight to Jesus. A conversation ensued, much like the conversation Jesus had with Martha, including the retort, "Lord, if thou hadst been

---

35 John 11:16.
36 John 11:17.
37 John 11:20.
38 John 11:21–22.
39 John 11:23.
40 John 11:24–26.
41 John 11:27.
42 John 11:28.
43 John 11:31.

here, my brother had not died."⁴⁴ When Jesus saw Mary weep, "he groaned in the spirit, and was troubled."⁴⁵ "Where have ye laid him?" Jesus asked. "They said unto him, Lord, come and see."⁴⁶ Upon seeing the tomb, "Jesus wept."⁴⁷

At the tomb, Jesus saw a great block of stone laid over the opening of a deep vault-like cellar excavated in the limestone rock. Jesus said to them that accompanied Mary, "Take ye away the stone."⁴⁸ At His command, "Martha, the sister of him that was dead, saith unto him, Lord, by this time he stinketh: for he hath been dead four days."⁴⁹ Jewish tradition held that by the fourth day, decomposition had begun. Nevertheless, in compliance with Jesus's desire, the great block of stone was removed "from the place where the dead was laid."⁵⁰

Jesus then prayed to His Father. "And when he thus had spoken, he cried with a loud voice, Lazarus, come forth. And he that was dead came forth, bound hand and foot with graveclothes: and his face was bound about with a napkin."⁵¹ Before the awestruck mourners, Jesus said, "Loose him, and let him go."⁵² Jesus did not roll the stone away from the entrance of the tomb or take the burial wrappings off Lazarus. Both tasks were performed by others. Jesus did what only the Son of God could do; He raised Lazarus from the dead.

The miracle of raising Lazarus was spoken of in villages and byways near and far. Some witnesses to the miracle "went their ways to the Pharisees, and told them what things Jesus had done."⁵³ Instead of being awestruck by the news, Pharisees and chief priests were troubled. They met together in "a council, and said, What do we? for this man doeth many miracles. If we let him thus alone, all men will believe on him: and the Romans shall come and take away both our place and nation."⁵⁴

In reasoning, Jewish leaders revealed their tenacious guard of Judaism and the law. Not only did they not believe the miracles of Jesus, but they also contended that the influence and power of Jesus threatened their way of life

---

44 John 11:32.
45 John 11:33.
46 John 11:34.
47 John 11:35.
48 John 11:39.
49 John 11:39.
50 John 11:41.
51 John 11:43–44.
52 John 11:44.
53 John 11:46.
54 John 11:47–48.

and their authority in the Holy City. They viewed followers of Jesus as seduced by miracles, which, if not stopped, would lead them to rebel against Rome. The high priest Caiaphas concluded for public safety, "It is expedient for us, that one man [Jesus] should die for the people, and that the whole nation perish not."[55] From that council forward, plans were laid at the highest levels of Judaism to put Jesus to death.

Knowing the mounting malice directed toward Him, Jesus left Bethany and His friends—Mary, Martha, and Lazarus. He journeyed to Ephraim, an isolated hillside town about fifteen miles northeast of the Holy City.

***

In the passing of my Grandmother Taylor, a miracle took place. Grandmother was dear to me. As she aged, she lost all ties with reality. She had no idea who I was. At times she called me Norma, my mother's name, or Esther, her sister's name. One time, she called me Fred, Grandpa's name.

The night of her passing, amid the pain and uncertainty of crossing through the veil, a miracle happened—a miracle that only I was aware of. As I took my grandmother's hand, she looked up at me and for the first time in years called me by my name. "Oh, Mary Jane, I'm so glad you've come. I've been waiting for you." That moment will always remain suspended in time for me. At her viewing, I wanted to weep openly but did so in the restroom, for everyone else was saying it was a blessing she could pass. I alone was selfish enough to miss her.

—Mary Jane Woodger, professor of Church history and doctrine at BYU

---

55 John 11:50.

CHAPTER FOUR
Jesus Commands the Elements of Nature

THE LAWS OF NATURE FAIL to explain how Jesus turned water into wine, walked on waves, calmed a raging storm, and withered a fig tree. Such miracles lie beyond the scope of natural law and beyond the power of man to comprehend without a testimony of the power of Jesus. Such events are an interference with nature—an interruption—not a break or change of the law.

TURNING WATER INTO WINE
John 2:1–11

St. John tells of Jesus attending "a marriage in Cana of Galilee."[1] Most Biblical scholars suggest the marriage was of a farmer. A few claim it was the wedding of a family member of Mary and Jesus. Even fewer point to it being the marriage of Jesus. Conjecture over whose marriage it was does not negate the presence of Jesus, His disciples, or His mother, Mary, at the feast.

At the wedding celebration, "when they wanted wine, the mother of Jesus saith unto him, They have no wine."[2] There is no explanation given as to why Mary was concerned about the lack of wine or why she felt responsible for providing wine for the guests. Gospel writers do not say that Mary explicitly asked Jesus to intervene. Her statement is declarative, informing Jesus about the lack of wine, nothing more. Yet "Jesus saith unto her, Woman, what have I to do with thee? mine hour is not yet come."[3]

"His mother saith unto the servants, Whatsoever he saith unto you, do it."[4] Jesus requested of the servants "six waterpots of stone," which were traditionally placed at the door of the wedding festivities and used by guests

---

1 John 2:1.
2 John 2:3.
3 John 2:4.
4 John 2:5.

to wash hands and feet.⁵ Surely there were plenty of empty wine pots or bags available, but Jesus did not want the smaller vessels. The waterpots held "two or three firkins apiece," a firkin being about nine gallons.⁶ The combined six pots held between 104 and 144 gallons of liquid.

"Jesus saith unto [the servants], Fill the waterpots with water. And they filled them up to the brim."⁷ When the pots were at the brim, without so much as an audible command or invocation to His Father, Jesus performed a miracle. He turned water in the pots to fine wine.

Jesus then said to the servants, "Draw out now, and bear unto the governor of the feast. And they bare it. When the ruler of the feast had tasted the water that was made wine, and knew not whence it was: (but the servants which drew the water knew;) the governor of the feast called the bridegroom, and saith unto him, Every man at the beginning doth set forth good wine; and when men have well drunk, then that which is worse: but thou hast kept the good wine until now."⁸ St. John wrote, "This beginning of miracles did Jesus in Cana of Galilee, and manifested forth his glory; and his disciples believed on him."⁹

***

When I was a young mother of three children, I lived in Sweet, Idaho. We had a house, a barn, and seven horses. Inside the barn were ten tons of hay. One night, I climbed up the haystack to throw hay through an open window to horses waiting outside. As I tossed the hay, my ring hit the window ledge. I knew instantly that my marquise diamond had popped out of the setting.

I jumped down from the haystack, ran to the house, and announced to my husband, "My diamond is lost." He said, "Let's gather the children and ask the Lord to show us where the diamond is." I was hesitant, for what were the chances of finding a loose diamond in the hay or on the ground? We prayed and asked the Lord for help. With flashlight in hand, we went outside. We saw a tiny glimmer on a board between the barn and the ground. The Lord showed me a shiny miracle that night.

—Julie Ann Rogers, artist

---

5   John 2:6.
6   John 2:6.
7   John 2:7.
8   John 2:8–10.
9   John 2:11.

First Miraculous Catching of Fish
Luke 5:1–11

Two miracles of catching fish are presented in the synoptic Gospels. The first appears at the beginning of Jesus's ministry and the second, near the end.[10] Both miracles took place after a night of fruitless fishing on the Sea of Galilee, and in both, Peter had a leading role.

Gospel writers Matthew and Mark omit the miraculous catching of fish, choosing to emphasize Jesus calling fishermen Simon Peter and Andrew to "come ye after me, and I will make you to become fishers of men."[11] St. Luke begins his narrative "as the people pressed about" Jesus in great numbers, eager to "hear the word of God, [as] he stood by the lake of Gennesaret [Galilee]."[12]

Near where Jesus was speaking were owners of fishing vessels. Jesus "entered into one of the ships, which was Simon's, and prayed him that he would thrust out a little from the land."[13] Simon Peter, being already identified with the Master, was agreeable to the request and launched his ship into the Sea of Galilee. Jesus seated Himself in the ship. (Sitting was the customary position taken when delivering a discourse.) He then preached to the multitude lining the shore. The subject of His sermon is not known. What is known is that "when he had left speaking, he said unto Simon, Launch out into the deep, and let down your nets for a draught."[14] Peter, who had spent long hours in the night trying to catch fish but without success, pointed out the futility of such action. But out of respect for the Master, Peter added, "At thy word I will let down the net."[15] Note, the command was to let down "nets" (plural), yet Peter replied in the singular.

"And when they," perhaps a reference to Peter and Andrew, "had this done, they inclosed a great multitude of fishes: and their net brake."[16] Peter signaled for his fishing partners, James and John, to come to their aid. The draught of fish filled two fishing vessels. "When Simon Peter saw it, he fell down at Jesus' knees, saying, Depart from me; for I am a sinful man, O Lord. For he was astonished."[17] Peter reacted to the miracle out of fear, knowing that Jesus

---

10   See Luke 5:1–11; John 21:3–11.
11   Mark 1:16–17; see Matthew 4:18–19.
12   Luke 5:1.
13   Luke 5:3.
14   Luke 5:4.
15   Luke 5:5.
16   Luke 5:6.
17   Luke 5:8–9.

had power to control the fish of the sea. "Jesus said unto Simon, Fear not; from henceforth thou shalt catch men."[18] When Peter and the other fishermen "brought their ships to land, they forsook all, and followed [Jesus]."[19]

***

My patriarchal blessing promises me "a desire to do genealogical work." I work in large-scale historical data conversion. The company I work for has more than 4,000 employees in India, Bangladesh, Sri Lanka, and Singapore. About 20 to 25 percent of their workforce at any given time index genealogical data 24-7 (three shifts a day) for top global genealogical websites. I am the only employee in the United States and the only member of The Church of Jesus Christ of Latter-day Saints. When we bid on a contract, it is for anywhere from small sets of 100,000 keystrokes to a billion keystrokes. We have keyed in every US census, and all UK censuses from 1841 to 1901. We have keyed vital records from Brazil, France, Denmark, Puerto Rico, Poland, Germany, Ireland, Africa, Australia, China, Hungary, Italy, Switzerland, Estonia, Ukraine, and Sri Lanka, to name a few. Even though I deal with big data every weekday, I still index a few names every week on my own. I need the blessings for myself and for my family. I am a witness to the miracle that the promise given so long ago, "a desire to do genealogical work," is being fulfilled.

—Yvette Arts, vice president of business development at Intellectual Management Inc.

Calming the Storm
Matthew 8:23–27; Mark 4:35–41; Luke 8:22–25

The very day Jesus taught a multitude from a fishing vessel off the shore of Galilee, He calmed an unruly storm. The narrative began in the evening when the multitude had been sent away. Jesus said to His disciples, "Let us pass over unto the other side," meaning cross the sea.[20] No time was spent in unnecessary preparations. St. Luke simply states, "They launched forth."[21] Other disciples did likewise, for as St. Mark reports, "There were also with

---

18 Luke 5:10.
19 Luke 5:11.
20 Mark 4:35.
21 Luke 8:22.

him other little ships."[22] It is assumed the smaller vessels turned back to avoid the approaching storm as nothing further is said of them.

As Jesus and His disciples crossed Galilee, a great storm arose. "The waves beat into the ship."[23] As the storm intensified and waves splashed over the vessel, the ship and its passengers "were in jeopardy."[24] Even with experienced fishermen aboard, they were no match for the unrelenting waves. But there was One aboard ship who had power over the storm-tossed sea. He had found a place to rest near the stern and had fallen asleep on a pillow. Neither the boisterous wind nor the sea splashing over the ship awoke Him. But He was awakened by the cry of the disciples: "Master, carest thou not that we perish?"[25] Their cry was not a request for Jesus to calm the sea, but more of a protest against what they perceived as His indifference to their perilous situation. Their cry has been memorialized in the hymn "Master, the Tempest Is Raging"—

> Master, the tempest is raging!
> The billows are tossing high!
> The sky is o'ershadowed with blackness.
> No shelter or help is nigh.
> Carest thou not that we perish?
> How canst thou lie asleep
> When each moment so madly is threat'ning
> A grave in the angry deep?
> Master, with anguish of spirit I bow in my grief today.
> The depths of my sad heart are troubled.
> Oh, waken and save, I pray!
> Torrents of sin and of anguish
> Sweep o'er my sinking soul
> And I perish! I perish! dear Master
> Oh, hasten and take control![26]

Jesus did not speak to His disciples of the raging storm or of a watery grave. Instead, He asked two questions: "Why are ye so fearful? how is it that ye have no faith?"[27] With keeping their vessel upright of utmost concern, why did Jesus ask about fear and faith? The answer lies in the promise Jesus gave His disciples

---

22   Mark 4:36.
23   Mark 4:37.
24   Luke 8:23.
25   Mark 4:38.
26   "Master, the Tempest Is Raging," *Hymns*, no. 105.
27   Mark 4:40.

before they launched out into the deep. He said that they would "pass over unto the other side" of the sea.[28] Jesus did not say to launch out in the evening so they could perish in an unruly storm. He promised an arrival at "the other side."[29]

Without the disciples' response to His queries, Jesus "arose, and rebuked the wind, and said unto the sea, Peace, be still. And the wind ceased, and there was a great calm."[30] The disciples marveled at the miracle and said one to another, "What manner of man is this, that even the winds and the sea obey him!"[31]

***

When I was a student at BYU, some things weighed heavily upon my mind. I felt a prompting to read my patriarchal blessing. It had been years since doing so. As I was walking to my room to find the blessing, the telephone rang. It was my father calling from New Mexico. After a quick greeting, he said, "I had an impression to call and ask if you've read your patriarchal blessing lately." The feeling that overcame me at that moment can't be described. How did he know? I'm convinced it was the influence of the Spirit. I am in awe of God's grace that He would inspire a parent about my immediate needs.

—H. Bruce Payne, program administrator of BYU Education Week

Walking on the Water
Matthew 14:22–33; Mark 6:45–52; John 6:16–21

After Jesus fed five thousand men plus women and children on the plains of Bethsaida, there was an attempt to crown Him King of Judea. When the disciples concurred, Jesus "constrained [them] to get into a ship, and to go before him unto the other side, while he sent the multitudes away."[32] The disciples begrudgingly accepted the constraint and took passage aboard a ship. As for Jesus, He went "again into a mountain himself alone . . . to pray: and when the evening was come, he was [still] there alone."[33]

---

28 Mark 4:35.
29 Mark 4:35.
30 Mark 4:39.
31 Matthew 8:27.
32 Matthew 14:22.
33 John 6:15; Matthew 14:23.

Did the Savior know as He prayed to His Father that the disciples were "in the midst of the sea, tossed with waves: for the wind was contrary"?[34] The account of boisterous waves on the Sea of Galilee was not the first time Gospel writers described "a great wind that blew" upon the sea.[35] St. Matthew tells of "a great tempest in the sea, insomuch that the ship was covered with the waves."[36] St. Mark writes of "a great storm of wind, and the waves beat into the ship," and St. Luke tells of "a storm of wind on the lake; and they were filled with water, and were in jeopardy."[37]

On this particular night, the disciples toiled to keep the ship afloat. Jesus "saw them toiling in rowing . . . about the fourth watch of the night."[38] (Nights were divided into four watches of three hours each, the first beginning at six p.m.) Jesus "cometh unto them, walking upon the sea" in the fourth watch, sometime between three and six a.m.[39]

"When [the disciples] had rowed about five and twenty or thirty furlongs"—a furlong being a hundred and twenty paces or an eighth of a mile—"they [saw] Jesus walking on the sea, and drawing nigh unto the ship."[40] "They were troubled, saying, It is a spirit; and they cried out for fear."[41] Jesus calmed their fears and "talked with them, and saith unto them, Be of good cheer: it is I; be not afraid."[42]

Peter cried out, "Lord, if it be thou, bid me come unto thee on the water."[43] Impetuous Peter climbed over the boat and, in faith, walked on the unruly waves. "But when he saw the wind boisterous, he was afraid; and beginning to sink, he cried, saying, Lord, save me."[44] "Jesus stretched forth his hand, and caught [Peter], and said unto him, O thou of little faith, wherefore didst thou doubt?"[45] Hand in hand, Jesus and Peter entered the ship and "the wind ceased."[46]

---

34   Matthew 14:24.
35   John 6:18.
36   Matthew 8:24.
37   Mark 4:37; Luke 8:23.
38   Mark 6:48.
39   Mark 6:48.
40   John 6:19.
41   Matthew 14:26.
42   Mark 6:50.
43   Matthew 14:28.
44   Matthew 14:30.
45   Matthew 14:31.
46   Matthew 14:32.

Witnessing their Master walk on water and Peter's faltering steps, the disciples were amazed "beyond measure, and wondered."[47] Rather than embrace Jesus or ask how He defied nature by walking on the sea, they worshipped Him, saying, "Of a truth thou art the Son of God."[48] This is the first time the title "Son of God" was said of Jesus by the disciples.

***

As a child, I looked forward to the yearly summer bike ride to the lake with Grandpa. Grandpa, always wearing a plaid flannel button-up shirt, would lead my siblings and me down a beautiful winding trail, teaching us safety signals and plant names. Grandpa always made it a special day. He passed away in my teenage years.

Though the memory of pedaling behind my grandpa grew hazy with time, I knew he kept an eye on me. A miraculous reminder occurred last summer after I had an argument with my brother. Tensions had flared, and I set out on a run, hoping to defuse my frustration. As I ran, I grew more incensed about the situation. I was almost fuming when I saw out of the corner of my eye an older man wearing a plaid button-up shirt riding a bike and waving for two young children riding bikes to cross the street.

I was instantly aware that the man and the children were not there by chance. As the trio rode out of sight, a lump in my throat formed. I knew that the scene was a gentle prod for me to expand my myopic perception beyond insignificant frustrations and remember the eternal scheme of life. I know that miracles occur regularly and demonstrate God's presence in my life.

—McKenna Swindle, graduate student at the Hebrew University of Jerusalem

Paying the Tribute Coin
Matthew 17:24–27

The Apostle Peter was asked by a tax collector, "Doth not your master pay tribute?"[49] The fact that the inquiry was made suggests a question in the collector's mind as to whether Jesus was subject to the religious tax, for rabbis were exempt. The collector's question had nothing to do with paying a civil

---

47   Mark 6:51.
48   Matthew 14:33.
49   Matthew 17:24.

tax to Rome or the collection of tolls or duties on goods. It was simply a religious tax.

Most were willing to pay the tax. After all, the tax supported costs associated with the temple—incense, priestly robes, oil for lamps, etc. Although backsliders sought to escape the tax, since the days of Moses the tax—a half shekel—had been extracted from every Israelite male twenty years and older.[50] (A half shekel is equivalent to about thirty-three cents today.)

Before Peter could inform Jesus of his encounter with the tax collector, the Master asked, "What thinkest thou, Simon? of whom do the kings of the earth take custom or tribute? of their own children, or of strangers?"[51] Peter answered, "Of strangers."[52] Jesus said, "Then are the children free."[53] His reply assured Peter that they were free from paying the religious tax. But then Jesus said to Peter, "Notwithstanding, lest we should offend them, go thou to the sea, and cast an hook, and take up the fish that first cometh up; and when thou hast opened his mouth, thou shalt find a piece of money: that take, and give unto them for me and thee."[54]

Note, Jesus did not say "for us." Even with Peter, He kept a separate status. For example, Jesus used the phrases, "my Father and your Father" and "my God and your God."[55] The "piece of money" Peter was to find does not suggest the impoverished circumstance of Jesus or Peter.[56] If they were penniless, Peter could have cast a net into the sea and obtained fishes enough to sell for the tax.

In humility, Peter went fishing with a hook and a line, much like he must have done as a young boy. The "piece of money" was in the mouth of the first fish to take his bait. The coin was a stater, a silver coin valued at sixty-six cents today.[57] The miracle was Jesus's knowledge that there was a fish in the sea with a stater in its gullet and that fish would take Peter's hook.

***

---

50 Exodus 30:11–16.
51 Matthew 17:25.
52 Matthew 17:26.
53 Matthew 17:26.
54 Matthew 17:27.
55 John 20:17.
56 Matthew 17:27.
57 Matthew 17:27.

When books are written describing how the world's genealogy records were gathered electronically into one great collection, the story will include many miracles. Here is one that happened to me.

As I first began working on what is today Ancestry.com, I contacted venture capital firms in Silicon Valley. The hobby of genealogy didn't register with any of the mostly young, mostly male investors. Although discouraged, I never lost my dream of creating "free intranets" for every family in the world to share family history, photos, and documents. A domain was acquired and a team in Utah went to work building technology to make my dream a reality.

Investor response was immediate—$13M in 1998, $33M in 1999, and $30M in early 2000. When the bubble burst in April 2000, funding dried up. Ancestry.com didn't adjust to the new reality. By the end of 2000, the company, now based in San Francisco, was out of funds, and talk of a hostile takeover or bankruptcy was being floated. This was agonizing to me. I sought the Lord's help. I went to the company headquarters in San Francisco and talked to each board member about a plan to bring Ancestry.com back to Utah, promising new funding from Utah investors. When the board voted, it was 7-0 in favor of the Utah plan with two abstentions. Within a few months, the company moved to Utah and the miracle of new funding from Utah investors was realized.

—Paul B. Allen, founder of Ancestry.com

Cursing of the Fig Tree
Matthew 21:18–22; Mark 11:12–14

As Jesus and His disciples were walking from Bethany to Jerusalem, St. Mark tells of Jesus being hungry. Jesus saw "a fig tree afar off having leaves," even though it was not the season of fruit.[58] It was springtime—Passover time. Jesus knew fig trees in Palestine did not produce fruit in spring—only in June, August, and winter. Yet in His hunger, Jesus hoped this tree was an exception. After all, its leafy facade had the appearance of having borne fruit. (Fruit-buds of the fig tree appear sooner than leaves. When the tree is in full foliage, the figs are well-advanced.) Expecting to find edible figs on the tree, Jesus "came, if haply he might find any thing thereon."[59]

When the Master and His disciples reached the tree, they were disappointed. There were no kermouses—green pear-shaped fruit—hidden under the broad leaves. There was nothing more than leaves hiding old figs from the

---
58 Mark 11:13.
59 Mark 11:13.

prior season. Jesus said to the tree, "No man eat fruit of thee hereafter for ever. And his disciples heard it."[60]

The next morning as Jesus and His disciples again passed the tree, "they saw the fig tree dried up from the roots."[61] Peter said to Jesus, "Master, behold, the fig tree which thou cursedst is withered away."[62] "And when the disciples saw it, they marvelled, saying, How soon is the fig tree withered away!"[63] The curse and subsequent withering of the fig tree is unique among the recorded miracles of Jesus. All other miracles have attendant blessings, not an attendant judgment. Symbolism attached to the cursed fig tree points to the house of Israel. In rabbinic lore, the fig tree symbolized the nation of Israel—a nation that Jesus watered, nourished, pruned, and expected to bear fruit.

Cursing of the fig tree was also the basis of an object lesson on the power of faith. Jesus said to the disciples, "Verily I say unto you, If ye have faith, and doubt not, ye shall not only do this which is done to the fig tree, but also if ye shall say unto this mountain, Be thou removed, and be thou cast into the sea; it shall be done."[64]

The withered tree also sets the stage for the parable of the fig tree—

> A certain man had a fig tree planted in his vineyard; and he came and sought fruit thereon, and found none.
>
> Then said he unto the dresser of his vineyard, Behold, these three years I come seeking fruit on this fig tree, and find none: cut it down; why cumbereth it the ground?
>
> And he answering said unto him, Lord, let it alone this year also, till I shall dig about it, and dung it:
>
> And if it bear fruit, well: and if not, then after that thou shalt cut it down.[65]

***

I studied the death mask of Hyrum Smith before selecting a man to portray him for a photo shoot on the martyrdom. One morning, between being asleep and awake—a type of dream state—I saw a man who looked very

---

60   Mark 11:14.
61   Mark 11:20.
62   Mark 11:21.
63   Matthew 21:20.
64   Matthew 21:21.
65   Luke 13:6–9.

familiar to me. He looked at me face to face, then turned to the side to show his profile, then turned to the other side to show the same. His bone structure was almost identical to Hyrum's death mask. I told my husband about the man and together we concluded he was in our stake. It was Richard Wilson. I telephoned Richard and asked him if he would portray Hyrum Smith for a photo shoot. "As it so happens, I have just returned from Nauvoo," Richard said. "On the trip my children said, 'Dad you look just like Hyrum Smith.'"

—Liz Lemon Swindle, commissioned artist for *The Chosen*

Second Miraculous Catching of Fish
John 21:4–11

Two miracles show Jesus's power to facilitate a large catch of fish. The first occurred early in His ministry when Peter was told to cast his net into the deep sea. Three years later, the second miracle occurred when the Resurrected Lord told the disciples to cast their net on the other side of the ship. Looking at the miracles together, the first marks the beginning of Jesus's ministry and the second signals the completion of that ministry.

The story of the second miracle begins with eight Apostles in Galilee. Their return to Galilee was prompted by the words of an angel to the women at the empty tomb and the words of the Resurrected Lord, who promised to meet them in Galilee. The Gospel narrative has Peter saying to his fellow Apostles, "I go a fishing."[66] They replied, "We also go with thee."[67] The desire to go fishing suggests Peter and the other Apostles were uncertain as to what to do next. They had come to Galilee as instructed, but where was their Master?

After securing a fishing vessel, the Apostles toiled all night to catch fish, but their nets were drawn up empty. When the first rays of morning light began to fill the sky, the Apostles steered their ship to the shore. St. John tells us that "Jesus stood on the shore: but the disciples knew not that it was Jesus."[68] The Master called to them, saying, "Children, have ye any meat?" They answered, "No."[69] He instructed them to "cast the net on the right side of the ship, and ye shall find."[70] No explanation was given as to why fishing on one side of the ship

---

66 John 21:3.
67 John 21:3.
68 John 21:4.
69 John 21:5.
70 John 21:6.

would be better than the other. Yet they obeyed the instruction and cast their net on the right side and "were not able to draw it for the multitude of fishes."[71]

The Apostle John was the first to recognize the Master. He said to Peter, "It is the Lord."[72] "When Simon Peter heard that it was the Lord, he girt his fisher's coat unto him, (for he was naked,) and did cast himself into the sea."[73] The other Apostles, being about two hundred cubits from shore, stayed in the ship "dragging the net with fishes."[74]

"As soon then as they were come to land, they saw a fire of coals there, and fish laid thereon, and bread."[75] Their Master was preparing a meal for them. "Jesus saith unto them, Bring of the fish which ye have now caught."[76] To bring in the draught of fish, "Simon Peter went up, and drew the net to land full of great fishes, an hundred and fifty and three: and for all there were so many, yet was not the net broken."[77]

Ancient philosophers concluded there was significance in the number of fish in the net. Augustine surmised that 153 is the sum of numbers one to seventeen, which was the sum of the commandments—ten on the stone tablets and seven gifts of the Spirit. Jerome purported the 153 varieties of fish represented the harvest of the world. Cyril of Alexandria claimed that one hundred represented Gentiles, fifty Israel, and three the Trinity.[78]

***

In spring of 1999, my husband and I were directors of Media Hosting for the Church. As requested by the Utah Travel Council, at 9:00 on a weekday morning, we met a reporter from Korea named Rosa and her cameraman. "I would like to interview a Latter-day Saint family," Rosa said. "Would you arrange it please?" I explained to her the challenge of parents leaving work, picking up children from school, and being in downtown Salt Lake.

Yet as Rosa and her cameraman talked with two Korean sister missionaries inside the Salt Lake Tabernacle, I frantically searched Temple Square looking

---

71 John 21:6.
72 John 21:7.
73 John 21:7.
74 John 21:8.
75 John 21:9.
76 John 21:10.
77 John 21:11.
78 David Guzik, "John 21—The Restoration of Peter," *Bible Commentary*; eduringword.com.

for a family. When I saw a family leaving through the north gate, I hollered, "Wait! Wait!" They stopped. Catching up to them, I asked, "Are you members of the Church?" They nodded. I explained that I was hosting a woman from the Korean national television who wanted to interview a Latter-day Saint family. The young father turned to his wife and asked, "What do you think?" She shrugged as if to say, "It's up to you." He turned to me and said, "We would be happy to do that. I served my mission in Seoul."

While waiting for Rosa and her cameraman to come out of the Tabernacle, the young father saw a mission companion and his wife. When Rosa came out of the Tabernacle, I introduced her to two families. She interviewed them as they sat on the lawn near the Assembly Hall not knowing a miracle had occurred.

—Sidney Price, JustServe specialist for the Church

CHAPTER FIVE
Jesus Provides Food for Multitudes

JESUS PROVIDED FOOD FOR HUNGRY multitudes on two occasions. The first was on the plains of Bethsaida and the second, in one of the ten cities of Decapolis on the southeast shore of the Sea of Galilee. Distinct differences between providing food on the plains of Bethsaida and Decapolis nullify the commonly held belief that the two miracles were one and the same.

FEEDING THE FIVE THOUSAND
Matthew 14:13–21; Mark 6:30–44; Luke 9:10–17; John 6:1–15

Upon learning of the death of John the Baptist at the behest of Herod Antipas, Jesus and His disciples departed from Herod's domain. They voyaged across the Sea of Galilee to Bethsaida Julias, a grassy meadow plain in the dominion of Herod's brother Philip. There, in a picturesque desert-like setting, Jesus fed five thousand men plus women and children. Why feed the multitude? The obvious answer is that those who had come to hear Jesus were hungry. But there was more than one reason for the miraculous distribution of food.

The miracle of feeding five thousand begins with people running "afoot thither out of all cities, and outwent them, and came together unto him."[1] When Jesus saw the multitude coming to hear Him, He "was moved with compassion toward them, because they were as sheep not having a shepherd: and he began to teach them many things."[2] He taught "them of the kingdom of God, and healed them that had need of healing."[3] The people were so intent on hearing the word of the Lord and/or receiving and witnessing His miraculous power that they hesitated to retire from Bethsaida.

---

1   Mark 6:33.

2   Mark 6:34.

3   Luke 9:11.

"Send the multitude away, that they may go into the towns and country round about, and lodge, and get victuals," the Apostles said to Jesus, "for we are here in a desert place."[4] Jesus replied, "They need not depart; give ye them to eat."[5] Aware of the cost of feeding so many, the Apostles asked, "Shall we go and buy two hundred pennyworth of bread, and give them to eat?"[6] (Two hundred pennyworth was about the cost of eight months' wages for a common Jewish laborer.) The disciple Philip, who made his home in Bethsaida, explained that "two hundred pennyworth of bread is not sufficient for them, that every one of them may take a little."[7]

Fulfilling the request of Jesus to "give ye them to eat" was a directive beyond the capacity of the Apostles to fulfil.[8] Yet Andrew, the brother of Simon Peter, said to Jesus, "There is a lad here, which hath five barley loaves, and two small fishes: but what are they among so many?"[9]

Jesus was not deterred by the paltry number of loaves and fishes. He replied, "Bring them hither to me."[10] The simple peasant meal—barley being a staple grain of the poor—was brought to Jesus. Jesus then prepared the multitude to receive the simple offering. He directed the men to sit in companies on the green grass. The companies were organized "in ranks, by hundreds, and by fifties."[11] The organization was reminiscent of an earlier day when Moses organized the children of Israel. According to Jewish tradition, in such a setting, women and children stood or sat away from the men.

When Jesus "had taken the five loaves and the two fishes, he looked up to heaven, and blessed, and brake the loaves, and gave them to his disciples to set before them; and the two fishes divided he among them all."[12] The loaves and fishes were then distributed to the multitude. In so doing, the Master "[fulfilled] the Jewish tradition that the Messiah would signal His advent by repeating the miracle of manna."[13]

After the multitude had eaten and were filled, Jesus said to the Apostles, "Gather up the fragments that remain, that nothing be lost. Therefore they

---

4   Luke 9:12.
5   Matthew 14:16.
6   Mark 6:37.
7   John 6:7.
8   Matthew 14:16.
9   John 6:9.
10 Matthew 14:18.
11 Mark 6:40.
12 Mark 6:41.
13 Black, *400 Questions & Answers about the Life and Times of Jesus Christ*, 133–134.

gathered them together, and filled twelve baskets with the fragments . . . which remained over and above unto them that had eaten."[14]

The miracle at Bethsaida was not lost on the multitude. They were stirred with religious fervor. Many were convinced that Jesus of Nazareth was the Messiah and said, "This is of a truth that prophet that should come into the world."[15]

Although the miracle was grand and reminiscent of the days of Moses, when Jehovah provided manna from heaven, the multitude would soon be hungry again. They rejected the Savior's Bread of Life sermon, for that was not the meal they wanted. In many respects, the miracle of providing food signaled a crisis in the ministry of Jesus. Men on the grassy plains demanded Jesus be crowned King of Israel and lead them against the Roman oppressors. Jesus refused.

St. John tells us, "From that time many of his disciples went back, and walked no more with him."[16] St. Matthew wrote, "[Jesus] sent the multitude away" and insisted His Apostles get in a fishing boat to cross the Sea of Galilee.[17] As for Himself, Jesus "went up into a mountain apart to pray."[18]

***

A newly converted member was moving to Toulouse and called the sister missionaries to come pick up food he was leaving behind. "I just thought you might have a better idea of what to do with all this," he told us. And sure enough, we did.

We called a refugee we had met on the bus two weeks earlier who loved God and loved coming to church and reading the Book of Mormon. Life for him had been incredibly unstable as he tried to find security in a new country. He spent most of his time looking for his next meal.

When we arrived at his apartment with the boxes of food, he broke into tears and said in broken English, "My sisters, this is beyond my imagination." I knew that day God had orchestrated this miracle and that He has a plan for His children.

—Eliza Allen, BYU student

---

14 John 6:12–13.
15 John 6:14.
16 John 6:66.
17 Matthew 14:22.
18 Matthew 14:22.

Feeding the Four Thousand
Matthew 15:32–39; Mark 8:1–13

Of feeding the four thousand, Elder Bruce R. McConkie wrote,

> This miraculous feeding of the four thousand is not a mere duplication or repetition of the feeding of the five thousand which took place a short time before near Bethsaida. Then our Lord was mingling with his own kindred of Israel; now he is teaching other hosts who in substantial part, being inhabitants of Decapolis, are presumed to be Gentile. Then he was laying the foundation for his incomparable sermon on the Bread of Life; now he is prefiguring the future presentation of the living bread to the Gentile nations. And significantly, this mixed multitude from the east of the Jordan were more receptive, and took a more sane and sound view of the matchless miracle of feeding thousands by use of the creative powers resident in him, than did the members of the chosen seed.[19]

The miracle at Decapolis, where large crowds listened to the Savior for three days, began as "Jesus called his disciples unto him, and said, I have compassion on the multitude, because they continue with me now three days, and have nothing to eat. . . . And if I send them away fasting to their own houses, they will faint by the way: for divers of them came from far."[20]

With this, the stage was set for the miracle. His disciples reasoned, "Whence should we have so much bread in the wilderness, as to fill so great a multitude?"[21] Had the disciples forgotten that Jesus fed an even greater multitude on the plains of Bethsaida with only five loaves and two fishes? The disciples remembered yet wondered whether Jesus would provide food for a multitude of Gentiles as He had for the seed of Abraham.

No matter their musings, "Jesus saith unto them, How many loaves have ye? And they said, Seven, and a few little fishes."[22] Jesus asked them to give of their food. To their credit, the disciples were willing to give their meager holdings. Jesus then "commanded the people to sit down on the ground: and he took the seven loaves, and gave thanks, and brake, and gave to his disciples

---

19   Bruce R. McConkie, *Doctrinal New Testament Commentary,* 3 vols. (Salt Lake City: Bookcraft, 1976), 1:375.
20   Matthew 15:32; Mark 8:3.
21   Matthew 15:33.
22   Matthew 15:34.

to set before them; and they did set them before the people."[23] "And they did all eat, and were filled: and they took up of the broken meat that was left seven baskets full."[24]

Like feeding the five thousand, more leftovers were gathered at the end than were prepared at the beginning. This was truly a miracle, for "they that did eat were four thousand men, beside women and children."[25] This time when Jesus sent the multitude away, there was no display of unbridled enthusiasm to crown Jesus the King of the Jews. The multitude dispersed without a disturbance. As for Jesus and His disciples, they "took ship, and came into the coasts of Magdala."[26]

***

My miracle is about my third-great-grandparents, Robert and Mary Henderson, who joined The Church of Jesus Christ of Latter-day Saints in Scotland. In his confirmation blessing, Robert was promised that he would gather with the Saints in Utah. The promise deeply troubled him, for he was a poor miner and saw no way the blessing could be fulfilled.

A few years later, the mining company asked for bids to dig a new air shaft. Although Robert had no tools or experience in digging a shaft, he submitted a bid. His bid was selected. Robert borrowed a pick and a shovel and started digging to reach the mine shaft below. When he was ready to quit and could no longer throw dirt out of the hole, he struck a crack in the earth that extended all the way to the mine shaft. The crack sent a burst of air into the mine. With funds received for digging the air shaft, in 1863 Robert and his family immigrated to America and settled in Utah.[27]

—Kenneth L. Alford, professor of Church history and doctrine at BYU and colonel in the US Army (retired)

---

23 Mark 8:6.
24 Matthew 15:37.
25 Matthew 15:38.
26 Matthew 15:39.
27 Family histories of Robert Henderson and Mary Ross Henderson, in the possession of BYU Professor Kenneth L. Alford, Colonel, US Army (Retired).

CHAPTER SIX
Jesus Passes Unseen

Jesus passed unseen before and after His Resurrection. In the first instance, angry men in Nazareth took Him to the brow of a hill, determined to hurl Him from the rocky cliffs to the abyss below. He passed "through the midst of them [and] went his way."[1] In the second instance, the Resurrected Lord was breaking bread with two disciples, whom He had met on the road to Emmaus, when He vanished out of sight.[2]

Passing Unseen in Nazareth
Luke 4:16–32

Jesus passed unseen among a boisterous crowd in his hometown of Nazareth. He was not a stranger to many in the crowd. They had known Jesus in His childhood and youth and watched Him grow to maturity.

St. Luke began this narrative as Jesus "came to Nazareth, where he had been brought up: and, as his custom was, he went into the synagogue on the sabbath day, and stood up for to read."[3] In synagogue worship, reading from the Law and the Prophets was expected. When a learned visitor entered the synagogue to worship among the villagers, the visitor was often asked to read from the Prophets.

Jesus was handed "the book of the prophet Esaias."[4] He read from Isaiah 61:1–2: "The Spirit of the Lord God is upon me, because the Lord hath anointed me to preach good tidings unto the meek; he hath sent me to bind up the brokenhearted, to proclaim liberty to the captives, and the opening

---

1 Luke 4:30.
2 See Luke 24:31.
3 Luke 4:16.
4 Luke 4:17.

of the prison to them that are bound; to proclaim the acceptable year of the Lord." Jesus did not finish the second verse, which describes His Second Coming. Instead, "he closed the book, and he gave it again to the minister, and sat down."[5] Although His role as a reader had ended, "the eyes of all them that were in the synagogue were fastened on him."[6] Jesus said to them, "This day is this scripture fulfilled in your ears."[7]

The initial reaction was wondering "at the gracious words which proceeded out of his mouth. And they said, Is not this Joseph's son?"[8] In other words, they asked, isn't this the son of Joseph the carpenter? Surely He could not be the long-sought-for Messiah. The assembled were "eager for a sign, a wonder, a miracle" as proof of His messianic role. "They knew that Jesus had wrought such in Cana, and a boy in Capernaum had been healed by His word; at Jerusalem too He had astonished the people with mighty works. Were they, His townsmen, to be slighted? Why would He not treat them to some entertaining exhibition of His powers?"[9]

Knowing their thoughts, Jesus said, "Ye will surely say unto me this proverb, Physician, heal thyself: whatsoever we have heard done in Capernaum, do also here in thy country. And he said, Verily I say unto you, No prophet is accepted in his own country."[10] Jesus reminded the worshippers of "many widows . . . in Israel in the days of Elias, when the heaven was shut up three years and six months, when great famine was throughout all the land."[11] The prophet blessed a gentile woman of Sarepta in Sidon and cleansed Naaman the Syrian.[12] Rather than rejoice in remembering the blessings the Gentiles received, the worshippers were "filled with wrath."[13] The scriptural examples implied that God loved the Gentiles, and the unspoken request for a miracle was denied.

Worshippers on that Sabbath day turned into a mob. They seized Jesus and took Him to the brow of a hill, determined to hurl Him from the rocky

---

5   Luke 4:20.

6   Luke 4:20.

7   Luke 4:21.

8   Luke 4:22.

9   "Chapter 16: Luke 4–8," *New Testament Student Institute Manual* (Salt Lake City: The Church of Jesus Christ of Latter-day Saints, 2002).

10 Luke 4:23–24.

11 Luke 4:25.

12 See Luke 4:26–27.

13 Luke 4:28.

cliffs. It was then a miracle occurred: "[Jesus] passing through the midst of them went his way."[14] The villagers had their miracle, but none saw it. The circumstances of that Sabbath day in Nazareth clearly illustrate the words of St. John: "[Jesus] came unto his own, and his own received him not."[15]

***

I was assigned to visit BYU–Pathway students in Accra, Ghana. As part of my visit, I was asked to deliver six laptops to some of our current students. I had heard horror stories about getting electronics through customs. Many electronics were held for ransom, tariffs, or just never seen again. Getting the wrong customs officer could be very costly. I could lose the laptops altogether, or even worse, I could personally be detained for questioning.

With a large suitcase in tow behind me, I approached the customs line. There was a customs officer standing in the middle of the aisle, and as people approached, he pointed at each person. One-by-one I watched every single person in front of me get pulled to the side so that their bags could be searched. As I walked up to the sorting area, it was as if the customs officer never saw me. I kept walking right past the officer and out the airport. I had not skirted the system. I did exactly what I was supposed to do. Everyone in front of me and, as far as I could tell, everyone behind me was pulled aside. The Lord had prepared the way for me to walk unseen so that I could deliver the laptops to faithful students in need.

—J. D. Griffith, vice president of administration at BYU–Pathway Worldwide

Appearing to Two Disciples
Luke 24:13–35

On the very day that the Lord Jesus Christ was resurrected, two of His disciples departed from Jerusalem on a road to Emmaus, a village about "threescore furlongs," or seven miles, from the Holy City.[16] As the disciples walked, they spoke "of all these things which had happened"—the Crucifixion of Jesus, the placing of their Master in a borrowed sepulchre, and the empty tomb.[17] "And it came to pass, that, while they communed

---

14 Luke 4:30.
15 John 1:11; see Isaiah 53:2–3.
16 Luke 24:13.
17 Luke 24:14.

together and reasoned, Jesus himself drew near, and went with them. But their eyes were holden that they should not know him."[18]

Jesus said to the disciples, "What manner of communications are these that ye have one to another, as ye walk, and are sad?"[19] The disciple Cleopas answered, "Art thou only a stranger in Jerusalem, and hast not known the things which are come to pass there in these days?"[20] In spite of darkness covering the sun, an earthquake, and renting the veil of the holy temple, had not this stranger heard of Jesus of Nazareth?

"What things?" Jesus asked. "And they said unto him, Concerning Jesus of Nazareth, which was a prophet mighty in deed and word before God and all the people."[21] "And how the chief priests and our rulers delivered him to be condemned to death, and have crucified him."[22] It was inconceivable to Cleopas that the stranger had not heard of the Crucifixion of Jesus of Nazareth, for word of His death had spread throughout the Holy City.

The disciples confided in the stranger their belief that Jesus "should have redeemed Israel: and beside all this, to day is the third day since these things were done."[23] They expressed their wish that Jesus had been the Messiah—the political/military leader to vanquish all enemies and rid the oppressed of Roman rule. As their conversation ensued, the disciples told of "certain women also of our company [meaning a disciple of Jesus] made us astonished, which were early at the sepulchre."[24] "And when they found not his body, they came, saying, that they had also seen a vision of angels, which said that he was alive."[25] Although the disciples had knowledge of Jesus and had heard that He was risen from the dead, they had lost hope.

It was then Jesus said, "O fools, and slow of heart to believe all that the prophets have spoken."[26] Jesus reviewed the teachings of ancient prophets: "And beginning at Moses and all the prophets, he expounded unto them in all the scriptures the things concerning himself."[27] As Jesus spoke, the two

---

18 Luke 24:15–16.
19 Luke 24:17.
20 Luke 24:18.
21 Luke 24:19.
22 Luke 24:20.
23 Luke 24:21.
24 Luke 24:22.
25 Luke 24:23.
26 Luke 24:25.
27 Luke 24:27.

disciples were reminded that truth does not come only by sight, but also by belief.

As the wayfarers "drew nigh unto the village, whither they went: [Jesus] made as though he would have gone further."[28] The disciples "constrained him, saying, Abide with us: for it is toward evening, and the day is far spent. And he went in to tarry with them."[29] The hymn "Abide with Me!" memorializes the disciples' request—

Abide with me! fast falls the eventide;
The darkness deepens. Lord, with me abide!
When other helpers fail and comforts flee,
Help of the helpless, oh, abide with me![30]

The disciples and the Resurrected Lord sat down together to partake of a simple meal, not a miraculous meal like feeding the five thousand on the plains of Bethsaida or the Last Supper in the Upper Room. It was in the breaking of bread that the disciples' "eyes were opened, and they knew [Jesus]; and he vanished out of their sight."[31] In wonder, the disciples "said one to another, Did not our heart burn within us, while he talked with us by the way, and while he opened to us the scriptures?"[32]

Straightway the disciples turned back to Jerusalem. Nothing was more important than to tell others what they had heard and seen—to give a confirming testimony that Jesus was resurrected.

***

When I moved to Chicago, I was a newly minted graduate student and about to become a mother for the first time. I wanted to find a job as a writer so that I could work at home when my newborn arrived. But where would I begin to find such a job in Chicago where I had no connections, no ins, and no prospects? I did the only thing I could think of in those days before the Internet. I turned to the Yellow Pages. I scanned and cold-called every book publisher, every newspaper, every magazine, and every company I thought might need a writer. The process took hours and hours and then days and days. The answer was uniformly, "No."

---

28   Luke 24:28.
29   Luke 24:29.
30   "Abide with Me!" *Hymns*, no. 166.
31   Luke 24:31.
32   Luke 24:32.

Then on a Tuesday afternoon after a Relief Society luncheon, as I was wheeling an overflowing garbage can to the dumpster in the back parking lot, I passed a phone on the wall in the hall. The phone rang. I answered. It was an editor from the *Chicago Sun-Times* wanting to do an article on Latter-day Saint women. After chatting for a few minutes, the editor gave me the assignment to write the story they wanted for their Sunday supplement. The chances that this would just happen are staggeringly low. Any other Tuesday afternoon, no one would have been at church, let alone me. I worked for the *Chicago Sun-Times* from that point on, and it opened the door to many other jobs for me.

—Maurine Jensen Proctor, co-founder and editor-in-chief of *Meridian Magazine*

CHAPTER SEVEN
Jesus Achieves Universal Miracles

OF THE MIRACLES OF JESUS, none has had a more universal impact than the Atonement and the Resurrection. Healing a blind man, calming a storm, and providing food for thousands had an immediate impact on individuals at the time of Jesus as did His walking on water and turning water into wine at the marriage celebration in Cana. The Atonement and Resurrection go well beyond the meridian of time. In a manner incomprehensible to mortal man, Jesus took upon Himself the burden of sorrow, suffering, and sin of all mankind from the days of Adam to the end of time and conquered death. The universality of the Atonement and Resurrection have bearing on us all. As beneficiaries of the universal miracles, we will rise from the dust of the earth free from the shackles of sorrow and sin to be with our loved ones and our Father in Heaven.

PERFORMING THE ATONEMENT
Matthew 26:30; Mark 14:26; Luke 22:39; John 18:1

Jesus, with eleven of His Apostles, walked from the Upper Room through the Holy City "over the brook Cedron" to the Mount of Olives, a mile-long chain of hills about three hundred feet from Jerusalem.[1] They climbed up the prominent summit known as Mount Scopus, which in Greek means "lookout point" and in Hebrew "mount of the watchman."[2]

Upon reaching the Garden of Gethsemane on Mount Scopus, Jesus left eight of the Apostles near the entrance with instructions to "sit ye here, while

---

1   John 18:1.
2   Black, *400 Questions & Answers*, 190.

I go and pray yonder."[3] He took "Peter and the two sons of Zebedee"[4] to a secluded area of Gethsemane. After they had gone a short distance, Jesus "began to be sorrowful and very heavy."[5] He said, "My soul is exceeding sorrowful, even unto death: tarry ye here, and watch with me."[6]

Denying Himself the companionship of His beloved Apostles, Jesus withdrew "from them about a stone's cast [a hundred feet], and kneeled down, and prayed."[7] St. Matthew tells us, "[Jesus] fell on his face, and prayed, saying, O my Father, if it be possible, let this cup pass from me: nevertheless not as I will, but as thou wilt."[8] St. Mark penned, "Abba, Father, all things are possible unto thee; take away this cup from me; nevertheless not what I will, but what thou wilt."[9] This was the "appointed hour—the hour for which he came into the world; the hour when he would take upon himself the sins of the world. For this purpose was he born; for this purpose had he lived."[10]

When Jesus arose and returned to Peter, James, and John, He found them sleeping and "saith unto Peter, What, could ye not watch with me one hour?"[11] Jesus admonished Peter to "watch and pray, that ye enter not into temptation: the spirit indeed is willing, but the flesh is weak."[12] Jesus left the chosen Apostles a second time and "went away . . . and prayed, saying, O my Father, if this cup may not pass away from me, except I drink it, thy will be done."[13] The word *cup* is a metaphor meaning that which is allotted by God, whether blessing or judgment.[14]

When Jesus returned a second time to the Apostles, "he found them asleep again, (for their eyes were heavy)."[15] They made no attempt to answer why sleep had overtaken them, "neither wist they what to answer him."[16]

---

3   Matthew 26:36.
4   Matthew 26:37.
5   Matthew 26:37.
6   Matthew 26:38.
7   Luke 22:41.
8   Matthew 26:39.
9   Mark 14:36.
10 Black, *400 Questions & Answers*, 192.
11 Matthew 26:40.
12 Matthew 26:41.
13 Matthew 26:42.
14 See Psalms 16:5; 116:13.
15 Mark 14:40.
16 Mark 14:40.

Jesus left them again "and prayed the third time, saying the same words."[17] Luke reported this time, "There appeared an angel unto him from heaven, strengthening him. And being in an agony he prayed more earnestly: and his sweat was as it were great drops of blood falling down to the ground."[18]

In that unselfish act in which Jesus took upon Himself our burdens of sorrow and sin, the Great Deliverer made sacred the Garden of Gethsemane, for in that garden He descended below all things to rise above them all. Jesus suffered the pain of all men, that all men might repent and come unto Him, for as Isaiah prophesied, "All we like sheep have gone astray; we have turned every one to his own way; and the Lord hath laid on him the iniquity of us all. . . . Surely he hath borne our griefs, and carried our sorrows."[19]

"And when he rose up from prayer, and was come to his disciples, he found them sleeping for sorrow."[20] In compassion, Jesus said, "Sleep on now, and take your rest: behold the hour is at hand, and the Son of man is betrayed into the hands of sinners."[21] In other words, there was no further reason to stay awake. Jesus had taken upon Himself the bitter cup and had borne the grief and sorrow of all mankind through the ages. In the distance, a band of men led by Judas was pressing forward to the garden. Standing with His Apostles, Jesus awaited the traitor's kiss.

***

"In the work of the Lord there is no such thing as a coincidence," said Elder David A. Bednar.[22] As a stake president, I am a witness to the truthfulness of his inspired words. I have seen miracles in my years of service. For example, I became aware of a sister in our stake who was in need and had the impression that I should reach out to her and put her in touch with another sister. I set up a meeting with the two women. The sister in need was reticent but agreed. As the women talked in my presence, resistance was evident until the sister willing to help said, "In my patriarchal blessing, I was told that I will reach out as an angel of light to those in need." It was then the sister in need said, "My blessing tells me that I will be ministered to by angels on both sides of the veil." In that

---

17 Matthew 26:44.
18 Luke 22:43–44.
19 Isaiah 53:4, 6.
20 Luke 22:45.
21 Matthew 26:45.
22 David A. Bednar, *One by One* (Salt Lake City: Deseret Book, 2017), 9.

moment, we all knew that the Lord was the God of miracles and that the day of miracles had not ceased.

—Brent B. Ward, director of Oral/Head and Neck Oncologic & Microvascular Surgery at the University of Michigan at Ann Arbor

Leaving the Open Tomb
Matthew 28:1–8; Mark 16:1–11; Luke 24:1–12; John 20:1–18

Jesus was taken from the cross and "laid . . . in a sepulchre that was hewn in stone, wherein never man before was laid. And that day was the preparation, and the sabbath drew on."[23] At the end of Sabbath "came Mary Magdalene and the other Mary" with the mother of James and Salome "to see the sepulchre."[24] The women brought with them "sweet spices, that they might come and anoint" the body of Jesus.[25] As the women drew near the burial site, they asked each other, "Who shall roll us away the stone from the door of the sepulchre?"[26] The issue was real, for the women didn't know that soldiers standing guard at the tomb had become "as dead men" when an angel rolled "the stone from the door" or that the soldiers had fled.[27]

When the women arrived at the sepulchre, "they found the stone rolled away. . . . And they entered in, and found not the body of the Lord Jesus."[28] The women were perplexed and frightened when they saw "two men [standing] by them in shining garments."[29] Rather than flee like the soldiers, they "bowed down their faces to the earth."[30] The angels asked them, "Why seek ye the living among the dead? He is not here, but is risen."[31] Addressing the frightened women, an angel said, "Fear not ye: for I know that ye seek Jesus, which was crucified."[32] "He is not here: for he is risen, as he said. Come, see the place where the Lord lay. And go quickly, and tell his disciples that he is

---

23 Luke 23:53–54.
24 Matthew 28:1.
25 Mark 16:1.
26 Mark 16:3.
27 Matthew 28:2–4.
28 Luke 24:2–3.
29 Luke 24:4.
30 Luke 24:5.
31 Luke 24:5–6.
32 Matthew 28:5.

risen from the dead; and, behold, he goeth before you into Galilee; there shall ye see him: lo, I have told you."[33]

Mary Magdalene was the first to bring word of an empty tomb to the disciples. "She runneth, and cometh to Simon Peter, and to the other disciple, whom Jesus loved, and saith unto them, They have taken away the Lord out of the sepulchre, and we know not where they have laid him . . . and told all these things unto the eleven, and to all the rest."[34] Her words were received as idle tales until Peter arose and ran to the tomb. The beloved Apostle John also ran. "So they ran both together: and the other disciple did outrun Peter, and came first to the sepulchre. And he stooping down, and looking in, saw the linen clothes lying; yet went he not in."[35]

Whatever prevented John from entering the tomb was no barrier for Peter. Peter went inside "and seeth the linen clothes lie, and the napkin, that was about his head, not lying with the linen clothes, but wrapped together in a place by itself. Then went in also that other disciple, which came first to the sepulchre, and he saw, and believed."[36] The two Apostles then "went away again unto their own home" to add their witness of the empty tomb.[37]

Of those who knew of the empty tomb, it was Mary Magdalene who first saw the Resurrected Lord. As she "stooped down, and looked into the sepulchre," she saw "two angels in white sitting, the one at the head, and the other at the feet, where the body of Jesus had lain."[38] The angelic beings asked, "Woman, why weepest thou?"[39] She answered, "Because they have taken away my Lord, and I know not where they have laid him."[40]

When Mary turned back from the sepulchre, she "saw Jesus standing, and knew not that it was Jesus."[41] The Resurrected Lord asked her, "Woman, why weepest thou? whom seekest thou?" Thinking him a gardener she said, "Sir, if thou have borne him hence, tell me where thou hast laid him, and I will take him away."[42] It was not until the Resurrected Lord said her name that Mary

---

33 Matthew 28:6–7.
34 John 20:2; Luke 24:9.
35 John 20:4–5.
36 John 20:6–8.
37 John 20:10.
38 John 20:11–12.
39 John 20:13.
40 John 20:13.
41 John 20:14.
42 John 20:15.

recognized Him and cried, "Rabboni; which is to say, Master."[43] Jesus said to her, "Touch me not; for I am not yet ascended to my Father: but go to my brethren, and say unto them, I ascend unto my Father, and your Father, and to my God, and your God."[44]

Jesus was seen in the Palestine area from time to time for forty days after His Resurrection. Only a few of His appearances were recorded by Gospel writers, who wrote that He appeared to:

- Disciples on the road to Emmaus, a village eight miles from Jerusalem.[45]
- Peter in or near Jerusalem.[46]
- Ten Apostles and others at Jerusalem.[47]
- Eleven Apostles at Jerusalem.[48]
- Apostles at the Sea of Galilee.[49]
- Disciples on a mountain in Galilee.[50]
- Five hundred men.[51]
- Eleven Apostles on the Mount of Olives.[52]

It is symbolic that Jesus was last seen on the Mount of Olives, where He had descended below all men to atone for the sins of the world, and now ascended above all men to return to His Father in Heaven.

Those who saw the Resurrected Lord could not be restrained from sharing the glorious news of His Resurrection, even if it meant imprisonment or worse. From city courts to rural byways, disciples spoke of Jesus Christ. The honest in heart listened and rejoiced in the knowledge that death was conquered and Jesus had won the victory.

***

---

[43] John 20:16.
[44] John 20:17.
[45] See Mark 16:12; Luke 24:13.
[46] See Luke 24:34; 1 Corinthian 15:5.
[47] See Luke 24:36; John 20:19.
[48] See Mark 16:14; John 20:26.
[49] See John 21:1–23.
[50] See Matthew 28:16–18.
[51] See 1 Corinthian 15:6.
[52] See Luke 24:50–51.

In the spring of 2017, I requested help with Swedish parish records from personnel at the Salt Lake Family History Library. A few weeks later, a researcher reported, "Your ancestors definitely wanted to be found!" She found the birthdate of Anders Gustav and information on Jan O. Nordvall, Per Sundin, Anders Gustaf Wallgren, Lisa Greta Persdotter, and others. She concluded her report, "I know you probably didn't expect your question to turn into a research project, and I really should have talked to you before proceeding further—I just got excited as your ancestry kept rolling out and rolling out and wanted to keep the momentum going."

Her kindness and expertise in answering my request was a tender mercy for me and for my ancestors who now have their temple work submitted.

—Shauna C. Anderson Young, professor emeritus of microbiology and molecular biology at BYU

CONCLUSION

"Have miracles ceased because Christ hath ascended into heaven?"[1] My answer and that of my friends mirror Mormon's reply, "Nay; neither have angels ceased to minister unto the children of men."[2] Sherilee Wilson, owner of Wilson Audio Specialties, knows with certainty that in 1984 when she was driving a Dodge van at night through a lonely strip of desert in Nevada, a distinct impression came to her—"What would you do if you got a flat tire?" She thought of different strategies, such as not breaking, slowing down, moving to the side without a jerking motion, and so forth. Sherilee recalled, "Within seconds, I had a flat tire. Instead of panicking, I calmly moved through the steps I had just rehearsed." Matthew Hyde, assistant director of For the Strength of Youth Program at BYU, also recognized a miraculous impression: "My wife and I dated over the phone. We talked about everything and fell deeply in love. However, when we traveled to meet each other, it was tricky. I got 'cold feet' when it came to talking about marriage. We broke up. Four months later, I had the simplest, purest thought—'I love her and should ask her to marry me.' I saw in my mind the ring that I would buy for her. She said, 'Yes!'" For Mary Ann Andrus, a mother of ten children, when her twelve-year-old daughter made poor choices, she prayed for a miracle. Mary Ann said, "Miraculously, my daughter recognized that she was on the wrong path. She currently serves in a stake Primary presidency."

None of these friends or others think their personal experience was anything but a miracle. Each was blessed with miracles great and small, much like the miracles in the days of Jesus. Jesus heard petitions of the blind, the lame,

---

1 Moroni 7:27.

2 Moroni 7:27, 29.

and of His mother, who wanted to quench the momentary thirst of wedding guests in Cana. No petition was too small for Jesus. President Russell M. Nelson's admonition in April 2021, "Learn about miracles," was not an idle request nor is the counsel to reflect on the miracles the Savior has wrought in your life.[3] For some, reflections stretch back to an event that set the course for a faithful life. Jeremiah J. Morgan, Deputy Attorney General for the state of Missouri, said:

> When I was fourteen years old, the Lord put in my life those who shared with me the fulness of the truths of the restored gospel. Of course, just because the Lord's timing was perfect does not mean it was easy. Like countless people before me, I had to exercise faith and face opposition. My mother, whom I count as one of life's greatest blessings, would not let me join the Church until I turned eighteen. I waited, for I had received an answer to my prayers. I had found my faith.

Glenn Rawson, writer and producer of *History of the Saints*, said:

> I was not raised in a religious home. In fact, if anything, I grew up despising the faithful. When I went away to college, I moved in with roommates who were members of The Church of Jesus Christ of Latter-day Saints. In time, because of their kindness, I was baptized. Looking back, I was neither converted nor repentant and scarcely believed in God, but I was headed in the right direction. Months following my baptism, I could not say that I had received an answer to prayer or that I knew much of anything. It was while reading the Book of Mormon that a thought came to me with great force: "That book is true!" Accompanying the voice came a feeling unlike anything I had ever known before.
>
> It was a warmth and light that seemed to cover me. That singular event more than forty years ago changed the course of my life.

And so it has been for millions of God's children through the generations. Miracles have blessed the lives of untold multitudes. For this, I am eternally grateful.

Are there other miracles we desire? Yes, but can we be content to wait upon the Lord? Like Elaine S. Marshall, a former dean of the College of Nursing at

---

[3] Russell M. Nelson, "Christ Is Risen; Faith in Him Will Move Mountains," *Liahona*, May 2021.

BYU, there are sorrows that still need to be washed away and deceptive cruelty to be resolved. But Elaine remembers, as do I, "God sends miracles when we least expect. We need only to notice."

ABOUT THE AUTHOR

Dr. Susan Easton Black joined the faculty of Brigham Young University in 1978 and taught Church history and doctrine until she retired to serve missions with her husband, George Durrant. She is the past associate dean of General Education and Honors and the director of Church History in the Religious Studies Center. For her research and writing, Susan has been the recipient of numerous academic awards. She received the Karl G. Maeser Distinguished Faculty Lecturer Award in 2000, the highest award given a professor on the BYU campus. Susan has authored, edited, and compiled more than 100 books and 300 articles.